CW00833359

CHELSEA'S

PERFECT
10

Sport Media
A Trinity Mirror Business

ABOUT THE AUTHOR

Neil Barnett has been writing, editing and broadcasting for Chelsea for over 20 years, having supported the team since 1959. He is currently *Chelsea TV's* senior reporter and presenter and is the on-pitch presenter at games.

His Chelsea jobs have been: matchday programme editor (1994-2004), club newspaper editor (1991-2004), telephone clubline reporter (1986-2005), on-pitch presenter (1992-present), *Channel Chelsea* television reporter (1998-2001), *Chelsea TV* reporter and presenter (2001-present), website news editor (2002-2006), matchday programme journalist (1990-2007), as well as various hosting and other jobs.

He is a Chelsea Pitch Owners vice-president along with Dennis Wise, David Webb, Ray Wilkins and Pat Nevin.

His biggest Chelsea regrets? The break-up of the 1960s team (1966); the break-up of the 1970s team (1974); the break-up of the promotion team (1977); the break-up of the John Neal team (1986); the break up of the Gullit/Vialli team (2001). And obviously all relegations and Cup exits.

Greatest Chelsea joys? Everything else.

Previous journalist work has seen him appear on BBC1, BBC2 and Channel 4, and he's been heard on BBC Radio 4 and various other stations. He's been a music editor in a London magazine, a sports editor in a London newspaper, run a London bookshop, and been unsuccessfully sued!!

But none of this is relevant as once he was able to embrace the drug of Chelsea it happily took over his life. Somehow, he is married with two children.

Sport Media
A Trinity Mirror Business

Published in Great Britain in 2008 by:
Trinity Mirror Sport Media,
PO Box 48, Old Hall Street,
Liverpool L69 3EB

Executive Editor: KEN ROGERS
Art Editor: RICK COOKE
Editorial Assistant: JAMES CLEARY
Cover Design: GLEN HIND

ISBN 978-1-905-26629-6

Printed and finished by Broad Link Enterprise Ltd

ACKNOWLEDGEMENTS

The players featured in this book are, or have been, amongst the very best in the world at what they do. There are not many people who can say that about themselves. Yet beyond their work and subsequent fame these players are all pretty regular human beings. I thank them firstly for that, and for all giving interviews specifically for the book.

I also thank them for their unique talents. Football is, rightly, the people's sport, a team game in which individuals can shine, especially if they put the interests of the team – the people – first.

Football has been a family game for me. My father took me to my first match and fell in love with Chelsea alongside me, continuing to go until his death in 2002. I apologise to him for not being able to fit in either Frank Blunstone or Eddie McCreadie, his favourite players. My mother started coming in 1970 and fell in love with Charlie Cooke. He remains her favourite. Tom and Caitlin, my children, had no choice but to attend and support and due to my work commitments with the club even my wife Mimi, whose roots had made her a Liverpool supporter, was reduced to taking the kids when they were young and suffered the Chelsea bug as well. I love and thank them all.

Two more thank yous. The fans: football will never exist without you, and all the players in this book have or had exceptional relationships with you. That is not coincidence. From publisher Trinity Mirror, James Cleary has been patient and supportive in the busiest of times.

CONTENTS

Perfect
10

PAGES

INTRODUCTION

I've got to tell the truth – this isn't the best book 'Spy' can write. He could come up with something far more controversial. After all, he's been behind the scenes at Chelsea forever, and he's seen it all and been told it all.

I've known him since I joined on associate schoolboy terms aged 14, and as the boys love and trust him, he's the one with the secrets! He's had the same relationship with management all that time as well.

But so long as everyone keeps on his good side, he'll keep his secrets and you'll have to make do with top entertainment like this. It's still bigger on insight that anything else you can buy. And if all goes well, it's the best you're going to get. Enjoy it!

John Terry
2008

Two who failed to make the cut – Roy Bentley (top) and Bobby Tambling (bottom)

NOT IN THE...

Perfect
10

William Gallas

To be honest, Willie should be featured in this book, but I want to sell it. No self-respecting Chelsea fan would buy a book listing as a Top Ten player the icon who turned his back on the club and went with bad grace to Arsenal.

So he's out!

It is a shame. In his time with Chelsea he was the best right-back, the best left-back and the best partner in central defence to John Terry. He could be a difficult personality – sometimes everyone was his best friend, sometimes the world was crushing his shoulders, and in his mind the grass was always greener somewhere else – but the players learned to love him and come kick-off he was capable of shrugging off injuries and psychological distractions and performing to the highest ability.

For five years Willie, many Chelsea fans loved you. You were brilliant. The Gallas-Terry central defensive partnership was the best in the club's history. But to get in this Top Ten you have to be loved still. It didn't have to end the way it did.

Winston Bogarde

Like many Chelsea fans, I have a Worst XI. Winston is left-back and captain. He was a decent, principled man who felt wronged after he had joined Chelsea and wasn't wanted, so I don't blame him for staying throughout his four-year contract and starting just four games. He was earning something like £2m a year. But the four games were pretty awful. So were his eight substitute appearances.

Ron Harris and Bobby Tambling

The club's record appearance maker, Ron "Chopper" Harris (795 games) and the record goalscorer, Bobby Tambling (202 goals) were outstanding servants and brought a lot of quality and, in Chopper's case, bruises to its history, but they get edged out by the sheer class of the chosen ones.

George Hilsdon, Hughie Gallacher, Tommy Lawton, Roy Bentley...

Before my time. I never saw them play.

Ruud Gullit

Did anyone change Chelsea more with his arrival than the dreadlocked Dutchman? This man wrote headlines. When he came, the world media came, and it has not gone away since.

After he had played three games, a 'mature' supporter came up to me at a reserve game and admitted: "I've seen Gullit play three matches and he's already in my Best XI." So many people felt like that. Manager Glenn Hoddle described him as looking like an 18-year-old playing with a bunch of 12-year-olds.

He has only just been edged out of the Top Ten. You need a

little more longevity than he gave to make it in there. But this guy is one top Chelsea legend.

Anyone in the 1980-81 team

This is the side which scored in just three of the final 22 League games of the season. Fans took to celebrating corners rather than goals.

Marcel Desailly

He won the World Cup and then joined Chelsea, bringing a totally new level of defending to the club. He stayed for six years and was often outstanding, especially in big games. But he wasn't better than Gallas who won far more, and again is just edged out.

Joe Sheerin

The shortest-ever Chelsea appearance, 30 seconds away to Wimbledon in 1997, the young centre-forward never even touched the ball. Having come through the youth-team ranks with the liking for a fag and a pint, and having once gone missing for three months, he was never really professional material.

But he later made a name for himself as an early captain of AFC Wimbledon where his skills stood out and his dislike for running was not such a major problem.

John Hollins, Alan Hudson and Peter Houseman

Three-quarters of the great 1970s midfield. Not everyone can get in.

Dan Petrescu, Roberto Di Matteo and Gustavo Poyet

Three-quarters of the great 1990s midfield. Again, not everyone can get in.

Michael Essien, Eidur Gudjohnsen and Claude Makelele

Members of the great 2000s midfield. Such anguish, but not everyone can get in.

Juan Sebastián Verón

Why did he come to Chelsea? After two years at Manchester United he hadn't learned English. He cost around £12.5m, played 14 games which included three substitute appearances, and managed in his one year to anger his manager, the fans... and me! He seemed a sulker.

He annoyed me when, after being away for five months (having announced he needed a back operation following an international abroad), he finally returned and agreed to do an interview for *Chelsea TV* to explain the course of events. He conducted it in Italian – not English, of course, and not in his native Spanish, but in the language of Serie A. However, before we started he was able to demand in English: "Only one minute!"

He is one of too many big-name or record signings who have flopped. But that makes him a perfect example of how hard it is to be a Chelsea Top Ten player.

LATE FOREWORD

Perfect
10

Tommy Docherty, Chelsea manager from 1961 to 1967, is knocking 80-years-old now. He is still a vibrant, iconoclastic, in-demand after dinner speaker. He recalls with great affection his 'Docherty Diamonds', the young Chelsea side he built around 1964 and 1965. He always recites it to a Chelsea audience. "Peter Bonetti, Ken Shellito, Eddie McCreadie, John Hollins, Marvin Hinton, the late Ron Harris... he's not dead, it was just the way he tackled!"

Well, in Tommy Docherty/Chopper Harris style this is the late foreword. By definition, it should come first. But I had to get my excuses and forethoughts out of the way over some of the people not chosen. Now I can tell you how I have chosen the Top Ten. I've cheated!

You have to set parameters in order to choose ten from the 642 players who had represented Chelsea come the end of the 2006-07 season. My first was to go with what I have seen. My first game was October 14th, 1959, a dull (as I recall) 1-0 win over Everton. The record books say Jimmy Greaves scored. I don't remember. I sat in the old double decker New Stand, as it was called, later the North Stand, and remember two goals being disallowed for offside (why do I remember them and not the real goal?). I recall Greaves taking corners below us and everyone chanting: "Chelsea!" and going 'thud-thud-thud' on the wooden floorboards, causing the stand to shake. So in the near-50 years since then, I decided to work through the decades.

Early 1960s

Jimmy Greaves.

1960s and 1970s

Peter Bonetti, Charlie Cooke, Peter Osgood. What about Alan Hudson? I started a standby list. Ray Wilkins went on it.

1980s

Kerry Dixon. Pat Nevin went on the standby list.

1990s

Dennis Wise and Gianfranco Zola. Half-a-dozen people went on the standby list. End of standby list!

2000s

John Terry, Frank Lampard.

That's nine players. Who could be my tenth? Petr Cech? No, I can't have two goalkeepers, that wouldn't sell the book. Bonetti or Cech? Cech is currently the best in the world, Bonetti is my first hero. Easy. Goalkeepers are different, they can be two halves. So we have eight-and-two-halves, and need one more. William Gallas? No, you'd stop reading now.

Then in a blinding flash it came to me. Actually, it came to me over a beer with Kerry Dixon while in Valencia reporting on the 2007 Champions League quarter-final, second leg.

I don't want the book to sell for two weeks, I want it to sell for two years. In two years' time, Joe Cole will definitely be in the Top Ten. If I want to keep this book contemporary, the man who is already deep in the hearts of Chelsea supporters must be included.

Later in the week I put this to him in exactly this manner. "You're not there in my Top Ten now, but I really think you will be in two years and you deserve a chapter!"

He looked at me with a child-like smile of delight. "In two years", he promised, "I'll be Number One!"

So, here we go. Chelsea's Eight And Two-Halves Plus One For The Future Top Ten – unless you're reading this in the future, in which case Chelsea's Nine Plus Two-Halves Top Ten.

Come on you Blues!

Neil Barnett

For Petes' sake - two great halves

Peter & Petr
Bonetti Cech

Petr Cech at six feet five inches (1.96m) is just one inch shorter than Chelsea's tallest ever goalkeeper and player, Ed de Goey. Peter Bonetti at five feet ten inches (1.79m) was just one inch taller than Chelsea's shortest ever goalkeepers, all of whom stopped playing well over 50 years ago.

Yet the similarities between Cech and Bonetti are far more striking than the differences.

Both made an immediate impact on getting into the team. Both have dominated their penalty area more than any other Chelsea keeper. Both have been unique in their handling of the ball. Both have made an impact on the world stage.

Chelsea's best goalkeeper in the first 50 years was undoubtedly Vic Woodley. He played throughout the 1930s and won 19 caps for England in an age when there were no tournaments to boost your total.

The most infamous goalkeeper before Bonetti was Chelsea's first, in 1905, Willie 'Fatty' Foulke. The six feet two inches, 22-stone monster was no laughing matter, an England international, but his Chelsea era spanned only one Second Division season.

In the first title-winning side of 1955, Chelsea used two goalkeepers almost equally – Bill Robertson and Charlie 'Chic' Thomson were solid rather than special.

Then came Bonetti. He made his debut as an 18-year-old in

1960 and kept his place for 19 years.

After him there were some terrific goalkeepers. Yet Eddie Niedzwiecki, Dave Beasant, Dmitri Kharine, Ed de Goey and Carlo Cudicini all peaked for only three to four years before injury, form or transfer dealings interrupted their seniority. Cech has simply raised the bar, the level of quality, effect, consistency and reliability.

Like Bonetti, he established himself when he was young, playing for Sparta Prague at 19. He came to Chelsea aged 22 in 2004. Chelsea has not stopped winning things since.

Petr Cech is not your average guy. He is a twin, and shared a bedroom with his twin sister until they were 16, having been born into the old Communist state of Czechoslovakia in a town called Plzen. By the time he arrived at Chelsea he had kept goal for Sparta Prague through a period when they didn't concede in the League for 900 consecutive minutes – 10 games – nor in the Champions League throughout his first four games in the competition. In all he had a period of 1200 minutes without letting in a goal.

He had won the European U21 Championships with the Czech Republic, saving twice in the decisive penalty shoot-out in the final against France after a 0-0 draw.

Following two years at Rennes in which he had plenty of work as they battled against relegation, he could speak fluent French. Within months of being at Chelsea his English was fluent.

Unlike most footballers, he doesn't require massive amounts of energy-storing sleep. Many top professionals are eight-to-ten hours a day sleepers. Petr hardly seems to need any. Instead he put his spare time during his first year at the club to studying, and in the summer of 2005 qualified for Prague University.

It was widely believed when Chelsea bought him that he

would have to start on the bench and find a way of taking a chance when presented one by the highly popular and impressive Carlo Cudicini. But Cudicini had a difficult pre-season with both fitness and form, and Cech went straight into the team under new manager José Mourinho.

Playing, however, wasn't enough for him. He wanted to understand the environmental foundations of Chelsea. "When I arrived, I wanted to know something about the club," he says. "I was looking for the best players, people who played for a lot of the years, and everywhere I found Peter Bonetti, the Cat.

"I'd never seen him play, I didn't know him, but everywhere I learned of his characteristics and him. You see 729 games for the club, it is unbelievable. It is quite incredible."

This is typical Petr Cech. He hasn't been prompted on Bonetti's statistic. The figure of 729, Chelsea's second highest appearance maker, is embedded in his mind.

I had the good fortune to be able to introduce them to each other for the first time when they appeared on a live Chelsea TV programme with me alongside Carlo Cudicini.

"He was really nice when I met him", says Petr, "it was really nice to meet him. He could speak about the differences between the past and now, but because he's been a goalkeeper coach he understands now really well. He was really interesting."

Since then they have met several times, including at the 2007 Chelsea Player of the Year awards when Bonetti presented him with the Special Achievement award for the way he returned to playing and top form so quickly after suffering a depressed fracture of the skull.

Peter Bonetti knew about Petr Cech before Petr knew about him. Peter had retired in 1979, but returned to Chelsea in 1983 as goalkeeper coach – the club's first ever – and continued his extraordinary relationship with the club until 1991. At this time he was also England's goalkeeper coach.

He became a freelance, based himself in Birmingham, and was attached to a number of clubs before settling at Manchester City for three years when Kevin Keegan was manager. That is where, in the new millennium, he discovered his finest successor in the Chelsea goal. His opinion of him now was set then.

"It's not changed since the first time I saw him," says the man the football world knows as the Cat, or Catty to his face. "I've told him myself. When he was 20, I saw him on a scouting mission playing for Rennes and the Czech Republic. The Czechs drew 1-1 with Holland and he was world class, he saved them.

"For a big man his reactions were fast, he could get down to shots. I liked his kicking, he had a good left foot. He came for crosses. He was first class. And he's got better with experience. I think he's the best in the world now."

That is something the International Federation of Football Historians and Statisticians have concluded. They first put Petr in at 10th in the world while he was at Rennes. At the end of 2004, after a few months at Chelsea, he had risen to second. In 2005 they voted him first. That same year he was voted Uefa's Most Valuable Goalkeeper.

"I rate goalkeepers over a period of a long time," says Peter. "I look for people who have been consistent for an era. Neville Southall, David Seaman, people like that. Now Petr Cech has been that for five years, and he still has a fantastic future.

"When players don't play for their team, you can often judge just how good they are. Well, Chelsea didn't play so well when they lost Petr with the skull injury. That is no disrespect to anyone who replaced him, but they weren't the same side."

Peter Bonetti was a revolutionary. He was different to other goalkeepers, especially other English goalkeepers, and he quickly became one of the all-time Stamford Bridge crowd favourites.

"My style helped," he says. "Because I was different from the normal goalkeepers, they called it the continental flavour. I had this flair of diving around, and I got the nickname."

Centre-forward Ron Tindall gave him that. The Cat. Catty. He thinks it was part of a confidence-boosting exercise, partly acknowledging his feline grace and outstanding agility, and partly relaxing his pre-match nervous energy.

The Cat had grown up in Worthing, Sussex, and the scouting network had missed him. Scouting was nothing like as national, let alone global, in those days as now. His parents had grown up in Putney, so they wrote to nearby Chelsea and asked if he could have a trial. Chelsea signed him when he was already 16.

"I had one full season in the juniors, and half-way through the following season I was called up to the first team. I'd played two reserve games."

In fact, England international Reg Matthews was injured, Bill Robertson was sick, and relegation-threatened Chelsea had to turn to the teenager. They'd lost their three previous games, conceding 10 goals. They'd won just three in 19, conceding 51. "I was playing at the Welsh Harp in the juniors one Saturday, and in the first team at Stamford Bridge the next Saturday."

Chelsea beat Manchester City 3-0 on his debut. Then they went to Arsenal and won 4-1. They lost 3-1 at home to title contenders Tottenham Hotspur on Good Friday, drew 1-1 at home to Nottingham Forest on the Saturday, and then went to White Hart Lane and effectively ruined Tottenham's championship challenge with a 1-0 win. Jimmy Greaves scored the goal, but 18-year-old Bonetti was man of the match with a series of phenomenal saves. So impressed was Tottenham captain Danny Blanchflower, later Bonetti's last Chelsea manager as a player, that he lined his side up to shake hands with the youngster on the final whistle.

At the end of that season Bonetti dropped back into the youth team to help them win the FA Youth Cup for the first time.

But that was it in the younger sides! He remained first choice goalkeeper when the following campaign kicked off, and was about to embark on a fast learning curve. Greaves moved on. Manager Ted Drake gave way and was succeeded by Tommy Docherty. Youngsters were introduced throughout the team, relegation was suffered, but promotion gained at the first attempt. From 1963, with the Cat now 21, Chelsea were a top side. And he was a top goalkeeper.

"Tommy Docherty was very good for me," he says. "I wasn't the most gregarious of people, I wasn't an extrovert. I was more of an introvert. But on the pitch I changed. I became volatile, talking, and I learned that from Tommy.

"He played in one of the early games, and I'll never forget the influence he had on me from a talking point of view. I was still a bit of a quiet keeper, and Tommy was telling everyone what to do. 'Your ball, Catty! Do this, do that!' And suddenly I realised the importance of talking to people and giving encouragement, and I became much more vocal on the field."

Docherty wanted Chelsea to be in tune with the 'swinging' 1960s. He changed Chelsea's kit to its still modern blue shirt, blue shorts and white socks. And he changed Bonetti into all green. "He wanted me to be different, to stand out. I was a shy lad. I wasn't one to go round talking to people unless they talked to me. But when the fans started chanting my name every game as I ran to the goal, I used to wave to them, and that is where it all started."

That is exactly where it all started. In the mid-1960s crowd singing and chanting was exploding massively, and here was the first footballer to respond and build a concrete relationship with the fans. Years later, almost everyone had their name chanted and just about everyone waved. But for a long time, Bonetti was the first and only one.

"The fans were fantastic. People said I was different because of my reactions and speed, and they took to me because of that."

In 1964 football arrived in people's homes on a weekly basis when the BBC launched *Match Of The Day*, and the Cat was an obvious stand-out personality on the field. Now, everyone talks of the importance of catching crosses. Then, Bonetti was setting the new trend. English goalkeepers punched, or stayed on their line. He was already prowling his 18-yard area, and was in full command.

"I found that I enjoyed that part of my game. If a ball was coming in I'd go for it. I knew with the right timing – it's all about timing – and with the agility to get up, and a bit of bravery – you have to come through bodies to get there – you can do it. The balls are lighter now, but it's still a question of confidence.

"A lot of times I used to see goalkeepers come and they were scared of falling, they wanted to land on their feet, and it didn't bother me that I caught the ball and ended up falling on the ground and rolling over. If they were rigid to stand on their feet, they'd get knocked and finish up dropping the ball."

So it was that one of the most familiar sounds from Chelsea supporters throughout the 1960s and 1970s was a howl of "No!" as Bonetti left his line to claim crosses, followed by an outburst of disbelief and intense applause when the ball was claimed and held.

In 1965 Chelsea won the fledgling League Cup. In 1966 they reached the semi-final of the Inter-Cities Fairs Cup, the precursor to the Uefa Cup, beating Roma and AC Milan along the way.

Certain outstanding saves became legendary. There was the

double save from Paul Madeley and Jackie Charlton in the final minutes of a 1-0 FA Cup win over Leeds United in 1966. That was on television. There was the upside down one from a Martin Peters header at home to West Ham, captured in photograph on the back page of almost every newspaper.

In that win over Leeds, Chelsea defended throughout after taking an early lead. Bonetti climaxed his outstanding performance by catching a corner on the edge of his 18-yard line in stoppage time. No punching or being glued to the goal-line for him.

How all of England was responding to 'swinging' Chelsea. On the hugely popular ITV television programme *Sunday Night At The London Palladium*, host Jimmy Tarbuck got the entire team, watching in the audience the night after the win over Leeds, to stand and take a bow. And then, as they sat down, he asked the Cat to stand and take his own personal bow.

That season he won his first England cap. He was in the England squad which won the World Cup. In 1967 he played in his first FA Cup Final and won Chelsea's first Player of the Year vote. In 1969, as he approached the then record of 402 Chelsea appearances by Ken Armstrong, he was voted by fans as Chelsea's greatest-ever player. "That was a great honour," he admits. "I was really, really chuffed about it. It was a wonderful achievement for me."

In 1970 he was runner-up in the Footballer of the Year poll, the first Chelsea player ever to be so recognised. Chelsea finished third for the second time in six years. Bonetti missed the home game against runners-up Leeds, and the away game at champions Everton, and if he suggested Petr Cech could be judged on how much Chelsea has missed him when absent, then that was the case in 1970. Chelsea lost both games 5-2.

But this was the year the team won the FA Cup for the first time. At Wembley, Leeds battered Chelsea, and Bonetti was in top form. He caught cross after cross on a muddy pitch, and made numerous saves. In the replay at Old Trafford, after suffering a bad injury, he played on and made more crucial saves. There were no substitute goalkeepers then. Today, he would have been replaced immediately.

On an unequalled night in Chelsea's emotional history, in an age when the FA Cup meant as much as the League, his injury brought serious anguish to Chelsea supporters. As full-time gave way to extra time, Chelsea's ten outfield players returned to the field, but he was still missing. He was having an injection. The Chelsea fans, along with 21 players and the officials, waited on tenterhooks to see if he would re-appear. On a night when lungs were hammered raw with singing, chanting and shouting, there was a significant silence followed, as he finally emerged, with no vocal sound at all. For some reason, there was just stunning applause.

It was the loudest applause I have ever heard at a football match. It was all the normal football things: love, worship, devotion and so on, but it was more. It was massive respect. It was a heartfelt thanks that the club's greatest-ever player, a decade now in the Chelsea goal, was still there. And he was still there at the victorious final whistle.

He had won six England caps, been on the winning side in every game, and conceded just one goal, when he was called upon in the quarter-final of the World Cup in Mexico. England threw away a two-goal lead against West Germany and lost 3-2, and despite making a couple of fine saves he was made the scapegoat. He was at fault for West Germany's first goal, but BBC commentator David Coleman demanded at one point he be knighted for his performance. Have another look at the goals conceded, and see what centre-half Brian Labone is palpable for!

But this is not the place to debate England. This is the place to pay homage to Bonetti's response. The following season he overcame crowd hostility at away games, "Bonetti lost the

World Cup" was constantly chanted. And he overcame two months out of the team with pneumonia to come back and be a crucial performer in the winning of the European Cup Winners' Cup over Real Madrid. It was Chelsea's first European trophy. Another of those outstanding saves, five minutes from time in the replay, a flying catch to Zoco's header, achieved legendary status.

By now, he wasn't only collecting medals and plaudits but going into another revolutionary field – goalkeeper gloves! He enjoyed this project.

"Now they are all-weather gloves. We had only wet-weather gloves. The ball sticks much better now and you get protection, they protect your fingers."

Goalkeepers were wearing woolly gloves, everyday gloves, when with a business partner he introduced ambidextrous cotton gloves – green, of course – with his name on them. For park goalkeepers they were brilliant, you could reverse them at half-time. For top goalkeepers they were better than the woolly ones, and soon over half the goalkeepers in the top flight were wearing Peter Bonetti gloves.

But if the 1960s and 1970s were the ages of youth, they were also the ages of early burn-out, and most footballers were expected to start packing their bags soon into their 30s. Bonetti was again the revolutionary.

As he got well into his second decade in the Chelsea goal, he showed that his game wasn't just reflexes and agility allied to good hands, good timing and bravery. With experience he relied increasingly on anticipation and presence. Wales international John Phillips emerged from the reserves, but couldn't replace him. Chelsea simply won more and kept more clean sheets with the Cat in goal.

"I was always a fitness fanatic. I wasn't a drinker. I played squash and badminton, and I was lucky, I didn't have many injuries."

The worst injury was probably a perforated bowel, suffered when making a save at the feet of a Bury forward in the League Cup in 1973. There were still no goalkeeper substitutes. Ten minutes after being carried off, he returned, bent over in pain, and finished the game. He was out for five months.

Relegation was suffered in 1975 as the club went near-bankrupt. Bonetti spent the summer in the USA where he was voted the thriving League's third-best player. Pelé was second. This was the same Pelé who in the late 1960s had said: "The three best goalkeepers in the world are Lev Yashin, Gordon Banks and Peter Bonetti."

But in 1977 promotion was again secured and Bonetti was still there, now nearer 40 than 30, the old man to a new young team featuring mostly homegrown players.

He played on for two more top-flight years, finally retiring at the age of 37. Those 729 games contained 208 clean sheets. Thirteen other goalkeepers had been used during his career, but none had amassed a significant total of games.

His final match, at home to Arsenal, was his 600th League appearance, and with his retirement announced both teams formed a guard of honour for him to run out through. In all this time, he had never had a goalkeeper coach. "Anyone would be better if they had a coach," he argues, "like in tennis and cricket.

"I started goalkeeper coaching at Chelsea. Ken Shellito was manager, it was 1978, the last year I was there. The kids were saying why can't we do something specific, and I started with them. Of course, I would have been better with a coach. That's why top clubs have full-time goalkeeper coaches now."

Similarly, there was no video of every minute of every game to replay action and correct mistakes. There was far less protection of goalkeepers by referees. And there were different pitches.

"By October you were squelching around in mud. If you were taking off to catch a cross, you didn't get a good run or leap. But you just had to get on with it. Now you don't have to worry about slipping over, lumps of grass here, mud there, the ball bobbling in front of you."

In 2005, Peter Bonetti was voted Chelsea's best goalkeeper of the club's first centenary by the fans. In a website vote, he was still in the top ten of best players in another vote.

In September 2006 he walked round the pitch at half-time against Liverpool to an ovation that only legends receive. He still turns out occasionally, now nearer 70 than 60, for Chelsea Old Boys.

Petr Cech followed his Czech record run of clean sheets with Sparta Prague by setting an English one with Chelsea in his first season.

The team went 1,024 Premiership minutes without conceding a goal – over 11 games. In the whole 38-game season, Chelsea's first champion season for 50 years, the team conceded 15 goals, an English top-flight record. He played in all but the last two games when the title was already won.

Before he was 25-years-old he had won over 50 caps. If he carries on at the same rate, he could be the first player in the world to win 200 caps.

It is difficult to compare his clean sheet record with Bonetti's. Football is so different. Bonetti had the likes of non-internationals Ron Harris and David Webb in front of him. Cech had Portugal's Paulo Ferreira and Ricardo Carvalho, England's John Terry and Wayne Bridge, France's William Gallas. But his clean-sheet ratio, nearly 55 per cent, is easily the best ever at Chelsea, and probably anywhere.

Early in the 2006-07 season, Chelsea were beating Liverpool 1-0 at Stamford Bridge and were down to ten men. Liverpool

were piling on the pressure, and there were five minutes of stoppage time. In the final one, an up-and-under cross was lumped in from near the centre-circle, and Cech came thundering out to leap and catch it above the jump of six feet seven inches Peter Crouch.

No punching, no sticking to his line. No handling doubts in the final seconds. It was so reminiscent of Bonetti 40 years before. No-one in the intervening years could do that. Chelsea won 1-0.

Petr pays homage to the players he works behind. "It's difficult to say in percentage terms who is most responsible for the clean sheets. It's very difficult to say, for example, for one clean sheet if the defenders deserve more praise or the goalkeeper.

"Every time, every game, the goalkeeper can make mistakes, and every time the defender can make mistakes, but if they work together very well there is always someone to cover. So it is important to play with good defenders and a good team, but the most important thing is understanding and command, and the way we play together.

"Of course, playing at Chelsea now with two of the best defenders in the world, Carvalho and Terry, and with great players on the right and left side, of course it helps."

He also pays homage to his manager, José Mourinho. "He is very important. If you have midfielders and strikers who stand and watch, who never defend well, what can you do? In this way a manager can help you. The goalkeeper plays with the system and the rest of the team, which with us defends as a team starting in attack. That makes everything much easier.

"As a goalkeeper you need to understand the way the manager wants to play. You have a lot of ball, and you need to know if you're playing a short game not to kick long balls, and you don't want to shout to organise another way defensively. You mustn't send players somewhere completely wrong.

"At Chelsea, everyone knows what to do and you've got quality players who know how to do it. The players are not robots, so they can always see how to correct situations."

It is clear Cech is a thinking goalkeeper as well as a massive one, a brilliant one, and therefore a virtually unbeatable one. But he is not a particularly loud one.

"You just have to say enough and that will do," he smiles. "I'm not the type of goalkeeper who speaks without stopping. I speak every time I feel the need. I need to be involved to keep everyone alert, or to alert someone of something.

"But it's much easier when you play with good players. You don't have to correct them every time. In my first team I spoke without stopping because the quality was different, I was having to correct players. It is much easier at Chelsea."

After establishing himself at Sparta Prague, he moved to Rennes in France at the age of 20. He chose that simply because it was the best offer on the table. He experienced two years of playing behind a struggling team, but for him they were two valuable years.

"If I'd stayed one more year at Rennes it would have been okay. I had a really, really good goalkeeper coach who taught me a lot. We addressed everything, every single game, every single training session. It was a good development time for me.

"But I felt that I was ready to step forward, to step higher to another level, and the offer came from Chelsea at the right moment."

He was reaching the top of his trade in his second choice work. His first choice had been to be an ice hockey goalkeeper, but it never materialised. "My father used to play ice hockey and was a good athlete. When he had to choose between both he chose athletics, and then played football as well.

"When we went to see my grandmother at the weekend,

she had a big garden with a little field. I tried every discipline, athletics, football, basketball, everything. I used to do every sport, I really liked it and still do.

"My favourite, number one, was ice hockey. I always wanted to be an ice hockey goalkeeper. I was taken by the club to join the Academy, but it was too expensive for our family, so I had to stay with football. That's why I play football. I'm not disappointed with that outcome now."

Petr's father used to cycle over from work to watch his training sessions. Now Petr can fly his family over to watch him play.

One adaptation that several goalkeepers have found difficult is when a different nationality of goalkeeper coach takes them over. Ed de Goey took time to adapt from British Eddie Niedzwiecki to Italian Giorgio Pellizzaro. Carlo Cudicini had a similar time changing from Pellizzaro to Portuguese Silvino Louro. But Cech had no problems when he arrived. And he had little problem adapting to the English game.

"It was really difficult sometimes," he claims. It certainly hadn't looked it.

"The first four games it was completely different. But I'd played in different teams, and that helped me adapt quickly. And at 19 I was playing for Sparta Prague where you have to win every game, you are under pressure every game, and Chelsea was exactly the same."

He has far less to do in a game than Bonetti had. One thing Silvino focused on in training was his concentration. Once again, you find that Cech is no ordinary man.

"During the game I don't feel like, oh I have to concentrate now because the ball is close. One hour before the game I've got in my head the system which is going on, and I only switch off when the game is finished. What I'm looking for during the game is just the pitch.

"I look only at the screen when I want to know the minutes

left on the clock. I stay all my concentration on the pitch.

"It is ridiculous, but it happens to me almost every time, there is a substitution and I don't know. We have a corner, and suddenly there is a player there who was not starting, and I'm saying, oh, what's happening here? But I'm so concentrated on the pitch.

"Sometimes I don't know who's scored because I'm concentrating on defenders, what if we lose the ball? I'm looking at the players behind to stop the counter-attack, or calling to players because there is a space.

"It's a little bit funny, but we won 2-0 away once and I'd not seen either scorer. I was asking afterwards who had scored the goals. They thought I was taking the piss."

In his first season he won the Carling Cup and Premiership. In his second he won the FA Community Shield and Premiership. In his third he won the Carling Cup and FA Cup. In his first and third he reached the semi-final of the Champions League.

In his first season at Chelsea he made numerous outstanding saves, and had two wonderful games in the Champions League, at home to CSKA Moscow and Barcelona. But in the latter game he suffered shoulder damage which restricted his movement the following season, and his second season was less phenomenal than the first.

He came back from surgery during the summer of 2006 in extraordinary time, after one full training session being restored to the team for the fourth game, and his form was dynamic. But in his eighth match he suffered a depressed fracture of the skull in the first minute at Reading when diving at incoming feet. He was seriously ill and sidelined for three months.

But, once again, his recovery was extraordinary, and as soon as the consultants cleared him to work he donned a head protector and took his place between the posts. There seemed no damage at all, not even temporary, to his performance.

He was outstanding in the FA Cup semi-final win over Blackburn Rovers, and then one of his important FA Cup Final saves against Manchester United was almost a carbon copy of the one through which he'd suffered the skull injury. He possessed no fear. His mental powers have been crucial. "I don't remember anything, so I don't think there will be a problem," he had said before his return.

He was playing Premiership and European football again before he was allowed to drive once more as he was on medication to protect him from epilepsy.

Being a serial winner has made him a special goalkeeper anyway, and he likes the pressures that brings. "It's difficult in the way everyone is looking at you and you can't make mistakes. But I really like the feeling of being looked at. If you're under pressure, if people demand a lot, you improve. It pushes you to the limits of your performance and concentration. It makes you better." When Mourinho and his management team left Chelsea, such was Cech's status that the club went and signed his treasured Rennes goalkeeper coach to work with him again.

In his first three seasons, despite the three months out, he played 126 games. At that rate he'll need another 14 to 15 seasons to catch up with Bonetti. That is unlikely, yet not impossible. Given his status, ability and professionalism, you wouldn't rule it out. In the first years of Chelsea's second century, it is almost certain that the best goalkeeper of this century has been playing.

Peter Bonetti on size counting

"No-one ever mentioned my size. In those days there were a lot of small goalkeepers, but in my case they'd say I made up for it with my agility. I had a lot more agility than the big guys.

Whenever I see Petr Cech I say if I had been your height, I'd have been a decent keeper! But whether that would have detracted from something in my game, speed, reaction, I don't know. You'd think it would help. Whether it would have coming out for crosses, I don't know. But maybe for shots just out of reach. But even then, would I have been so quick to get there?"

Petr Cech on size counting

"It's very important. In this moment with the development of the game, everyone is faster, quicker, bigger, the balls are flying much more than even five years ago – the balls are made for strikers to score goals – then when there is no time to react, the smaller goalkeepers who are agile with quick feet sometimes have no time to move their feet. That's when size matters. When you have a split second to make a save, you can't make steps to help yourself, you just reach. The bigger you are, the further you reach. On crosses too, you can catch them higher."

Neither goalkeeper likes to choose a best save. But under pressure, they both come up with one.

Peter Bonetti on his best save

"We beat CSKA Sofia 1-0 at home (in 1970). There was a header that came in from point-blank range. It was in the net, and I've somehow twisted back and hooked it out. I had just a split second to turn backwards and hook it away. I think that was one of my best."

Petr Cech on his best save

"I still think it was the one from Eidur (Gudjohnsen, a deflection from his team-mate following a corner at home to CSKA Moscow, 2004). He was really close and it was not what you expected. It was a miracle the ball went over. And equal with that, a save against Barcelona at home in that first year (in 2005), a header from Puyol that I kept out just on the line. It was really close in, and I still don't really understand how the ball stayed under my hand right on the line."

Most appearances for Chelsea

795	Ron Harris,	1961-80
729	Peter Bonetti,	1960-79
592	John Hollins,	1963-75 & 1983-84
445	Dennis Wise,	1990-2001
421	Steve Clarke,	1987-98
420	Kerry Dixon,	1983-92
410	Eddie McCreadie,	1962-74
409	John Bumstead,	1976-91
402	Ken Armstrong,	1946-57

Most Chelsea clean sheets
Up to the end of 2007-08 season, only starting games are measured.

208 in 729 games, 29%,	Peter Bonetti	1960-79
94 in 206 games, 46%,	Carlo Cudicini	1999-2008
90 in 166 games, 54%,	Petr Cech	2004-08
78 in 245 games, 32%,	Sam Millington	1926-32
77 in 239 games, 32%,	Jim Molyneux	1910-22
72 in 178 games, 40%,	Ed de Goey	1997-2003
60 in 272 games, 22%,	Vic Woodley	1931-45
55 in 175 games, 31%,	Eddie Niedzwiecki	1983-88
51 in 146 games, 35%,	Dmitri Kharine	1992-99

Born to lead

John
Terry

This is the tale of how a homegrown Chelsea youngster became the club's best captain and arguably its best player of all time. He became its most medalled player and the England captain. He went from, on the surface, being a quiet, uncertain young man with a massive inner determination, to being an up-front leader who is at his most powerful on the field of play. In fifty years time, when the fantastically successful Chelsea teams of the first decade of the twenty-first century have their reunions, John Terry will still be the captain. He'll still be the leader. He was born to lead.

John Terry knew exactly where he wanted to go, it was just a case of getting there. The 13-year-old terrier midfielder who loved a tackle was being wooed by several clubs.

There was his local team, West Ham; there was the side he supported, Manchester United; and from West London there was Chelsea. He had trained with all of them. Manchester United had wanted him so much they had sent their bright prospect who also originated from his manor, David Beckham, back south to watch him play and persuade him to move up north.

In the 1990s when you reached the age of fourteen, you could sign associate schoolboy terms with a professional club. Despite his family being West Ham supporters and it being local, despite Manchester United being the biggest club in the land and his 'club', young John had no doubts. It was to be Chelsea. When he had gone training at Chelsea he had felt most comfortable. It may have been run-down, it may not have been the big club it is now, but they encouraged him to play his football and he enjoyed himself.

So, Chelsea it was. He arrived with his parents just after his fourteenth birthday on a matchday, had lunch in the corporate lounge, and was due with them on the pitch at half-time to sign his forms. But his father, Ted, was not happy. He could see massive advantages in John joining Manchester United.

Ted has been a huge influence on the footballer and captain of Chelsea and England, John Terry. Ted was captain of Bardag, a team that played at a respectable level, and John used to watch him as often as possible. Leadership qualities seem to be in their genes.

It was my job to host the signing of the youngsters in front of the matchday crowd. I had fetched a table and chairs from the players' bar and stood them on the pitch, and was waiting at the mouth of the tunnel with my stadium microphone. But it became clear that Ted was determined the signing was not to take place. Father and son had it out behind the scenes. It was as passionate as you could imagine a Terry argument to be.

In the end, Chelsea called off the signing. If it wasn't the right environment, it wasn't worth trying to force through. But 14-year-old John told his father that his mind was made up, come what may he was signing for Chelsea at the next home game. And he did!

He took to the pitch at half-time with just his mother Sue and youth-team coach Graham Rix, and became a Chelsea associate schoolboy.

Things didn't go according to plan. In his last year at school, when he should have been playing for Chelsea's U16s, and when those of his colleagues who were hoping to become full-time Youth Training Scheme apprentices the next season were establishing themselves in the U18s side, he was mostly stuck on the substitutes' bench for the U16s.

It was a worrying period. Sitting now reminiscing in the massive changing room at Chelsea's Cobham training ground, his large home a mile away in Oxshott where wife Toni and their twin son and daughter live with him, it feels like he's squire of this manor. He is! But his journey to the top seemed very distant when he was sixteen.

"Coming up to YTS, I went through a stage at fifteen and sixteen when I didn't grow," he says. He speaks quickly, with authority. "I'd still got my puppy fat, and the players around me were becoming men. I hadn't fully developed, I'd got stuck, and my performances in that crucial year weren't as good as they should have been. I was a man in a boy's body. Physically, everyone was fitter, stronger and faster than me."

It got to May. He'd started four youth-team games by now and been a substitute four more times, but there was no hint of a YTS offer. Then, on May 6th 1997, his telephone rang.

"It was playing on my mind. Then right at the end of the season I got a call from Mick McGiven saying I'd been called up to the reserve-team squad." Gwyn Williams, in charge of youth development, had demanded he be involved in the final reserve game of the campaign to give him one more chance to prove he was good enough for Chelsea. It was away to Luton Town the next day. He was a substitute.

"We went from Harlington (Chelsea's old training ground) round the M25 in the minibus with me not knowing most of the players. I knew it could be my last chance. It was a chance for them to look at me against men."

The team was made up of first-team squad players who weren't going to be involved in that season's FA Cup Final, and of youngsters. It was a losing side. By the time John was introduced they were 5-0 down.

"I came on with about twenty minutes to go in central midfield. I scored one after about five minutes, a header, I'd made a good run into the box and got on a cross. I was delighted. I turned round but there was no-one there celebrating with me. But there were some senior players, Dave Lee, I think Dave Rocastle was playing, Paul Hughes who had made his
first-team debut, and they started saying: 'Brilliant JT…' I was JT back even then. Dave Lee and Rocky were brilliant with me. I was cleaning Dave Lee's boots the next year.

"About five or six minutes later, I popped up with another goal. I was getting on the ball and playing well. As we were going back to the centre-circle Dave Lee said to me: 'You're up front now!' and I said 'Mick McGiven has said I've got to play central midfield.' He just said: 'You're on a hat-trick, get up front!'

"I finished up in the hole behind the forwards, trying not to let either Dave Lee or Mick down. Dave was applying real pressure. He kept saying: 'Come on, we'll get you your hat-trick.' But I didn't have another shot. After the game Mick McGiven put an arm round me and said: 'Brilliant!' He was great to me as well. A couple of weeks afterwards I got offered my YTS agreement."

By the closest of margins, John Terry thus became a Chelsea player.

He was quiet, appeared shy, and most clearly he was uncertain when he didn't know what was right. You could see he needed to be doing the right thing. He was still a boy. And after the unimpressive season the year before, despite that reserve game, he wasn't selected for the first youth-team match of the season.

On September 13th 1997, John Terry's world, Chelsea

Football Club's world, and the England national team's world changed. Chelsea Youth won 3-0 at home to Barnsley.

"We were struggling for defenders and Ted Dale (the youth-team coach) said would I mind playing centre-half. We won and I got Man of the Match. I felt good. I liked seeing everything in front of me. I'd always read the game well, and seeing it all I coped really well."

He was playing sweeper in a back three, and he was beginning to grow fast. Immediately he was organising, encouraging, informing, as he took to the position. He was neither quiet nor shy, and never uncertain, on the pitch.

A month later Chelsea's youth team went up to Leeds and the 16-year-old John Terry did battle with 16-year-old Alan Smith. It was a terrific game and, not long after Smith scored, Terry went up the other end and scored himself. The great competitor was revealing himself. The match finished 3-3.

As the year thundered on with the first team always in the headlines, the manager changed from 'sexy football' Ruud Gullit to Gianluca Vialli and the League Cup and European Cup Winners' Cup were won, John Terry was becoming a man and very quickly a reserve-team player. On the pitch, he always felt comfortable.

"I led and spoke whenever I played, even though I was rarely captain. I went to the reserves and was a young player there. Maybe if I'd stayed in the youth team I'd have ended up captain there. In the reserves I wasn't telling experienced players what to do, but if they made mistakes I wasn't scared of speaking to them. They'd come to me after and say: 'That's great! We like all that.' They knew I respected them. But off the pitch I'd be scared to talk to them!

"I was in digs with Paul Nicholls (youth-team goalkeeper). We were being thrown into foreign territory. I was nervous away from home. My brother (Paul Terry, who did his YTS at West Ham and was released) said that after his two years YTS

he thought he could have worked and tried a lot harder. He
said to listen to the coaches, to learn, and to talk to them.

"I'd seen players my own age arguing back with coaches
and getting nowhere. I'd speak to coaches and see what they
wanted me to improve on. I had my chance in football and I
gave it everything in my body." He finished up the club's Young
Player of the Year.

His second season started in the reserves. By the end of
October, still aged seventeen, he had made his first-team
debut, coming on in the last five minutes of a League Cup tie.
He came on late in a League game in December, his Premier
League debut, to shore up midfield. He made his full debut in
the third round of the FA Cup at right-back, the first time in his
life he had played there. In March, he made his European
debut, also at right-back, setting up the opening goal for his
player-manager Vialli.

He was tall now, still slim and, although he wasn't fast, he
rarely seemed to be exposed. Famously, he had laid Vialli out
with a thunderous tackle in his first training session with the
first team.

In the summer of 2000, when record signing Jimmy Floyd
Hasselbaink joined, and when he was still a 19-year-old
youngster, he was deliberately fouled by the striker in their
first session. That session made the newspapers for an
argument between Hasslebaink and central defender Emerson
Thome. However, it didn't make them for the time out the
striker had to take for treatment after Terry had quietly taken
retribution on the expensive one, just to make sure there was
no foot being left in on this youngster again. John Terry knew
how to make his mark.

The boy was quickly becoming a man. "I remember sitting in
the meeting not knowing anything with my suit on," he says of
the Vålarenga game, his first in Europe, "expecting not to see
my name up even on the bench. I looked at the bench names

and mine wasn't there. It was two seconds after that I realised: John Terry, right-back. It was too close to the game to be shocked or nervous. Managerially, Luca played that very well, and when I crossed one in for him and he scored the opening goal I was very pleased. We won 3-2."

The following season his game picked up in the reserves. He was confident on the ball, hitting long passes with both feet, confident on his first touch. He was unlucky that the League Cup started with a home defeat to lower league Huddersfield. The defending was okay but the team couldn't score. At Sunderland in the Premiership when the side was 4-0 down at half-time he replaced Marcel Desailly and had a good second half, Chelsea finally losing 4-1. He got to play in the FA Cup again and scored his first goal for the first team at home to Gillingham, then cuddled a supporter in the Matthew Harding Stand because he couldn't think of another celebration! He'd already done okay in the Cup against Nottingham Forest, and with the March transfer deadline coming and them battling relegation from the Championship, called Division One at the time, he went out on loan. He was still nineteen.

"That was vital for me. I was in foreign territory again. Gwyn and Luca pulled me in the office and said it was a good opportunity to go. Luca said it would help me develop, that they were struggling and it was a chance to help them. Then he said, come back at the end of the season and we'll see where you are.

"I came back and was on the bench for the Cup Final! I still speak to Ricco (Graham Rix, former first-team and youth-team coach) about that now, he was pushing for all the young English players to be on the bench."

Terry started just five games for Nottingham Forest and came on in another – his first – and they went undefeated in all of them. By the start of the next season he was a

19-and-a-half-year-old man and the holder of an FA Cup winner's medal as Chelsea had beaten Aston Villa with him, Jody Morris and Jon Harley all on the substitutes' bench.

"When I first came in the team I was still on a fast development curve. I went from five feet seven inches to six feet two inches so fast, and then for a year I was like Bambi. I had these skinny long legs, a long body. I remember having chats with Ade Mafe and Antonio Pintus (fitness coaches) and they were saying it will take time but your body will adjust. They got me in the gym doing squats and weights."

That was helping with his pace as well, which was still a concern. Off the pitch he was beginning to gain confidence in the first-team environment, but found the support of kitman Aaron Lincoln crucial.

John Terry laughs heartily a lot of the time, but no-one can get him laughing more than Lincoln. "I did all his work!" he claims now. "My YTS duty included to look after the kitman, and me and Nicho did everything. We had to get in early each day before everyone else, seven-thirty, eight, and lay out the kit. Then after that we'd be in there having a cup of tea and watching telly with Aaron.

"We just formed a great relationship, he was just a great bloke." Terry would have Lincoln by his side early on if he was giving interviews to help him be funny, or just to give him ideas. Really, it was to ensure he was saying the right thing when he wasn't certain of his environment. Later, their relationship was to take on a completely new quality.

"I wasn't happy with my agent, Aaron had a new contract with Chelsea which was only a season, so he finished and gave it a go as my agent. He's done brilliantly for me. And he's done brilliantly with Chelsea because he's a mad Chelsea fan."

Having started convinced where he wanted to establish his environment, and having trodden with care through the new fields he had chosen, now he was building his manor. It was to become the biggest and strongest in the country.

The next stage was a problem. Chelsea's centre-backs were the existing World Cup-winning pair of Desailly and Frank Lebœuf. Emerson Thome was also in the squad and had been impressive since arrival. Christian Panucci had joined on loan from Inter Milan and Winston Bogarde had come in on a free transfer from Barcelona, and both could play centre-back.

Terry's game was improving fast, however. Jim Duffy, a seasoned Scottish central defender, had joined as youth-team coach and taught him how to tackle while at the same time ensuring you don't get hurt. McGiven was working on him tackling less recklessly.

Desailly privately told me at this time that Terry would play for England for a long period. He cited an England central defender whom he thought would struggle to get into other top national sides because of his lack of technique, and felt that the young Terry had the necessary technique and defending quality to go to the top.

Five League games into the new season, Vialli was controversially sacked and Claudio Ranieri became manager with a brief to regenerate the ageing team. John Terry started the season full of promise but with no clear path forward. He finished it winning the club's Player of the Year award.

"When Ranieri first came, Chelsea Reserves played Coventry Reserves at Stamford Bridge, and that night I played one of the best games I ever played for the rezzies. I caught Ranieri's eye. He was sitting with Ray Wilkins, and Ray pulled me the next day and said he'd been talking and asking about me."

Once again he got his chance in the League Cup, this time playing sweeper between Desailly and Bogarde at Anfield. Liverpool won after extra time. He was nervous, inhibited, but not out of his depth. Back in the reserves his game was developing at a pace. In the next couple of weeks both Panucci and Bogarde managed to fall out with Ranieri – or maybe the other way round – and Thome had moved on so, when Lebœuf was suspended at home to Derby County, Terry was selected at sweeper. He'd played the previous game in the absence of Desailly in a four-man defence with Lebœuf. Chelsea beat Derby 4-1, and for the next game at Middlesbrough Terry was selected ahead of the France World Cup winner, with Desailly.

Lebœuf returned for the injured Desailly next game, and Terry played on, blossoming fast. On Boxing Day 2000, when the team hadn't won away for nine months, they went two-up at Ipswich Town and were hauled back to 2-2. There was much wrong with the side. You could sense the long-term changes coming. Terry cleared two off the line, including one in the dying minutes.

"I remember playing well that day, and maybe it helped the manager stick with me for a run. Early on we soaked up pressure, I challenged for lots of balls and was winning crosses. We scored two, I cleared two off the line, one with my head, one late on. I was solid."

The changes came. Terry was a fixture for the remainder of the season, Lebœuf played less and less. In goal, Carlo Cudicini replaced Ed de Goey. Youngsters were used throughout the team: Sam Dalla Bona, Jody Morris, newly-signed Jesper Grønkjær, Eidur Gudjohnsen; plus another new signing, Slavisa Jokanovic.

"Frank Lebœuf was upset, understandably so because he was brilliant. But he had the decency to come to me and say: 'I'm angry, but not with you.' Those kind of things stick with you, a World Cup player left out but he comes and wishes you good luck before a game."

It wasn't a great team. When they went to title contenders

Arsenal in mid-January, standing ninth in the League, they were expected to lose. Indeed, the day before the team had practiced with a 4-4-2 shape in training, but for the match Ranieri selected a 3-4-3 shape. The question, whatever the shape, however, was how would 20-year-old Terry deal with the explosive pace of Thierry Henry.

If there was ever a match to define a youngster, this was it! The score finished 1-1.

"Henry was probably at his best, and this was one of the best games early in my career. I made some strong challenges early on, and scored a really good header." That equalised Robert Pires' early goal. "The game was live on Sky and I got man of the match. Next day in the papers it was all about me. I think that game represented a real test, and it was a breakthrough for me.

"I remember sitting next to the coach window looking up at Highbury after and realising I'd bitten my nails right down. I was really nervous. I still get nervous now, but once I'm on the pitch it's gone. It helps me get up to the concentration levels you need."

Terry had managed to marry his reading of the game to the pace he had and his strength, which was fast increasing; and to his power in the air and his always underrated technique, to live at the top level on his first test.

The Player of the Year award was a major accolade for him. "There were a lot of foreigners in the team and I think the Chelsea fans really enjoyed seeing me and Jon Harley coming through. They always had a song for us even if we weren't playing. I think they loved the way I played, throwing myself into tackles. When I got up to accept the award I was speechless. I still get stick about that now."

Chelsea finished the season sixth and qualified for the Uefa Cup. Lebœuf moved on along with Dennis Wise and Gustavo Poyet. The new era had arrived. It was to be led by new captain Desailly, and by old hands Zola and Graeme Le Saux, but the most established new era boy was the Player of the Year, John Terry.

William Gallas joined in 2001. By now Terry was England U21 captain. He hadn't been capped at a lower level, but everything was moving so fast. He'd scored his first national goal too.

"I was in a few U21s squads but not always in the team and then Howard Wilkinson moved on. Just before we played Finland away, Sammy Lee, who'd been number two, he came to my room. He said he was going to play me alongside Titus Bramble and make me captain. Sammy was a legend for me. I really enjoyed being with England."

At the beginning of the 2001-02 season he was fully a man. His game now was no longer stacked with potential. It had arrived. His personality had developed and he was comfortable on and off the pitch. The world was getting to know John Terry.

In early December, Desailly needed a spell out with tendonitis and Terry and Gallas, with Cudicini behind them, went eight consecutive games together in which they conceded just one goal. The greatest defensive partnership in the history of Chelsea Football Club was established.

In two of those games, each side of his twenty-first birthday, Terry captained Chelsea for the first time. They weren't great successes. They lost 1-0 at home to Charlton Athletic, the one goal conceded in the run in the last minute, and drew 0-0 at Sunderland thanks especially to a Cudicini penalty save.

Terry was excited immediately by the arrival of Gallas. "We were in Roccaporena (an Umbrian mountain retreat to which Ranieri took all his teams) when we first signed him, and I paired myself up to him for drills. We became quite close although his English was non-existent. It clicked from day one. On the pitch we worked well together. I liked to attack the ball, win headers, he was quick and read the game well. But he could go up and attack, he could go for headers, and I could come and sweep behind him."

Things couldn't have been going better or faster. Increasingly, he was living the fast life. He was a major personality in the squad now, he was a social organiser for the younger members of it, he was a man without fear. But that could get him into scrapes. On the night of Thursday January 3rd, two days before an FA Cup tie at Norwich City, he got arrested at a club in Kensington when drunk and charged with causing actual bodily harm and affray. The court case dragged on until the following season when he was found not guilty. CCTV footage proved his innocence. The charge was silly. However, being drunk in public under forty-eight hours before a game was unbelievably silly. He wasn't released from jail until after the team had travelled to Norwich for the match. The whole process was the biggest wake-up call of his life.

England dropped him immediately. There had been talk of a call-up to the full squad for the World Cup. There was the European U21 Championships. He missed out on the lot.

Crucial people stood by him. Girlfriend Toni drove him to the team hotel in Norwich on the Saturday morning, and then secreted him away after the game. He had a hand covered where he had broken a knuckle in the fight on the Thursday. Ranieri brought him on as a substitute at half-time and continued to play him. Chairman Ken Bates stayed close to him throughout the court process. The fans started chanting at every game on every occasion he did anything good: 'Terry for England.'

But from a man without fear, John Terry became someone very scared indeed. He knew if found guilty he could go to jail. He knew he was innocent, a victim if a stupid drunken one.

"I was never really a drinker," he claims now. "That was a night when I made a huge mistake and it's stuck with me ever since. It was a silly mistake and I won't make it again. Going to training after that was a relief. After, I was getting home and then going to the solicitors and watching videos of the event, and it was doing my head in because I knew I hadn't done anything wrong."

One other person stood by him who turned out to be crucially important: Gianfranco Zola. "Franco was the kind of guy to put an arm round you, talk to you, and he gave me just a few words, saying you can't be doing things like this. I spoke to Franco and Graeme (Le Saux) about it. And then Franco took me golfing with Hitchy (Kevin Hitchcock, former Chelsea goalkeeper who was now coaching at Watford), and we'd all have quite a chat and then go back to Franco's for dinner and I'd go home after that. They were changing my habits."

Two-and-a-half weeks after the arrest Chelsea got thumped 5-1 in the second leg of the League Cup semi-final at Tottenham. Terry was at fault for the early Spurs goal. Typically, he finished the game in attack chasing a consolation. He was experiencing a steep learning curve. It was to go on for almost another two years.

Chelsea's season hadn't improved on the previous one in the League. But in the FA Cup, the team marched to the final. In the fourth round they drew at home to West Ham, then won the replay 3-2. Terry headed the last-minute winner from a Le Saux corner. In the semi-final he scored the only goal of the game, squeezing home a left-footed shot from a tight angle. How he was becoming the main man!

"The West Ham game was big for me. All my family were there, I'd got them tickets in the West Ham end. I was looking through some photos the other day and found Lamps coming to give me a huge hug – he'd been getting stick off the crowd. It was a really good header.

"Fulham was a scrappy goal squeezed in. I ran off blindly, curved my way back to the halfway line, didn't know what to do, and then realised the Chelsea fans were on the other side of the pitch! I still hadn't worked out my celebrations!"

His technique now was making him stand out: the quality of his tackling, the touch, the use of his head, and more than anything the use of his chest – has there ever been a better 'chester' of the ball?

"I always was good at all that, especially tackling. In midfield I was at my best winning duels. I remember my dad drumming it into me as a lad, I'd play with my left foot for a day, I'd do keep-ups with my brother in the garden. I always wanted to be left and right-footed.

"I think with tackles it comes from my reading of the game. I might go and block the pass or block the attempt to pass me. If you go straight to the ball, the opponent might get a nick on it and finish up doing you. Making blocks on shots is a big thing as well. There was a game when I had a ball mark on my chest the day after. I got a big buzz out of that. I love all that."

But the season came to a desperate end when he awoke on FA Cup Final day and immediately fell over from a bout of dizziness. He had a bug which was affecting his ear and consequently his balance. He had to make do with being on the bench and coming on at half-time, but he wasn't fit and Chelsea lost 2-0 to Arsenal.

Then he picked up an injury in the pre-season of 2002-03 and Desailly and Gallas established themselves. He returned to the reserves at his own request to get going. "I was on a contract where if I played twenty games I could get a new deal, and I was thinking, would I play twenty games?"

The court case was finally behind him, and when Chelsea played Everton at home in the fourth round of the League Cup in early December, he started just his third match of the campaign. Despite Zola playing, Ranieri surprisingly made him captain and announced he was now vice-captain to Desailly. He was three days short of his twenty-second birthday. It was an extraordinary act of faith.

"I'd captained the rezzies in quite a few games, and the gaffer and the players knew what had been happening, and he said it was in my qualities to be a leader and a captain. I think Graeme Le Saux and Franco Zola were suggesting it too."

When he made his first Premier League start of the season ten days later in place of the injured Desailly, typically he scored the equaliser at Middlesbrough. He finished up playing twenty-nine games that year, rediscovered his form and it was no surprise when he won his first England cap.

Chelsea qualified for the Champions League, Roman Abramovich bought the club and bought virtually a new team, but he and Desailly started the following season as Gallas came back from a pre-season injury. Yet when the first Champions League game was played, away to Sparta Prague, he was left out along with Lampard and Eidur Gudjohnsen.

"I think we were all flying at the time. I'd established myself and was playing really well. At the team meeting, it was a tight room, and it was me, Lamps and Eidur sitting next to each other. The team went up and it was one of them…" he turns his head in disbelief. "…What's happened here! What are we *doing* here? We were all gutted.

"Willie came back in and he scored the winner so it was the right decision to put him in the back, but not with Lamps and Eidur. Lamps came on at half-time and changed the game."

At the next away Champions League game, a 4-0 win at Lazio, Terry was magnificent. At the highest echelon of club football, he looked a world-class player and captain. "Things stick in my mind from that night, the stadium, the goals. They had some good chances early on, Carlo made some brilliant saves. Willie cleared one as well. It was one of those nights when everything clicked." In two crucial minutes he back-flicked to safety an Inzaghi header that was falling for forward Corradi to strike, and then headed to safety a

Stankovic twenty-yarder rocketing towards the top corner. "There was a little bit of naughties with them in the tunnel before and after, and Mihaljovic spat at Mutu and got sent off soon after. Then Lamps had a volley which came back out and Eidur shot in. The three of us were doing the business. We made a statement that night not only as individuals but as the new Chelsea in Europe."

He was now playing regularly, either next to Desailly or Gallas. Indeed, a new problem was noticeable. He found it hard to produce his best form with Desailly. This was not because of the ageing Frenchman's play, but because he passed back the captain's armband. Leading, playing with uninhibited authority, was now an essential part of his game. John Terry had been born to lead, and when he wasn't in charge his game suffered.

In the third round of the FA Cup in January 2004 he was rested. Chelsea only drew 2-2 at Watford from the First Division (Championship). Terry had trained in the morning then gone and sat on the bench to support the team. It was typical of him. Most players would simply have taken the afternoon off. At his post-match press conference a frustrated Ranieri announced that the team could no longer play without Terry. At twenty-three years of age, he had become the foundation of the most expensively-assembled team in the world. In ten years he had reached where the 13-year-old boy wanted to go.

"The day before that game the manager asked me how I was feeling. He said I'd played a lot of games. I told him I was feeling good. He said he was going to rest me with a busy period coming up. I wasn't even to be on the bench, so I went to support, sat behind the dug-out. And after he said to me, 'never again,' if I'm fit I'll play.

"I got home and saw what he'd said to the press and realised it was a big statement. So long as I was playing well, I was playing."

Terry captained Chelsea in the Champions League quarter-final win at Arsenal and the semi-final at home to Monaco, when they went out that season. Then the man who had supported him almost all the way, Claudio Ranieri, was sacked.

"For me, he was brilliant. He gave me a break, a chance. Ted Dale put me at centre-back in the youth team and I'm still in contact with him, I've got a good relationship with him, Mick (McGiven) is still at the club, and Claudio gave me my first real chance. He was brave enough to do it with Frank Lebœuf still here. Not many managers would play you in front of a World Cup winner He had the balls to do it."

In his place José Mourinho arrived. The new manager said in a press conference that he needed a new centre-back. Terry, on holiday in Dubai, was startled. He telephoned me to see what I knew. It was typical of his uncertainty when he hits new ground and isn't the master of it. I told him Desailly was announcing the next day that he was leaving the club.

"I was lucky. Marcel was brilliant with me. Him and Frank both were when I came through. He'd talk to me, never for half-an-hour, but for five minutes walking in from training to the dressing room. He'd give me small details, and they're huge still when I look at the game now. He was funny in his ways. He'd sit there in the dressing room talking to himself, 'No, Marcel, this is stupid,' in his French voice, and then he'd turn to me, I was laughing, and he'd say, 'No, don't laugh, you can learn from this.' And I did."

It was no surprise when Mourinho made Terry captain. In the next three years he won and lifted: the Carling Cup and Alan Hardaker Award for Man of the Match in the Final (2005); the Premier League with a record low of goals conceded and a record high of points won (2005); the PFA Player of the Year (2005); the FA Community Shield (2005); Uefa's Most Valuable Defender (2005); selected in the FifPro World Team of the Year (2005); the Premier League (2006); Chelsea Player of the Year

(2006); selected in the FifPro World Team of the Year (2006); the Carling Cup (2007); the FA Cup (2007); and with Ronaldinho he became one of only two players to be selected for the first three FifPro World Teams of the Year (2007).

He played for England in the European Championships of 2004 and World Cup of 2006, being selected in the FIFA squad of the 2006 tournament, and became England captain.

In the first title season, 2004-05, Terry and Gallas played together in the centre of defence on eighteen occasions. They conceded one goal. With Petr Cech behind them and Claude Makelele in front, this was arguably the finest defensive diamond of all time anywhere.

"It was massive," Terry admits. "Big Pete was unbeatable in training. Everyone was saying you can't beat him, you can't score. He's worth twelve points a season! Maka was sweeping up, cleaning up, tidying up, he was great on the ball and strong, especially for so small a man. The whole defence got a lot of credit, but Maka played a huge part. Myself and Willie still really clicked. Even when he played left-back.

"In training, when José first took over, we had a game that finished 5-4 and José was going mad. 'How can your team score five and yours four?' That was his mentality. From then on training sessions were 1-0s and 2-0s."

When Gallas played left-back, Ricardo Carvalho was next to Terry, and the outcome was almost as good. "Riccy played pretty similarly to Willie, so we worked well together. He'd let me dominate in the air, he'd sweep up really well. When we had Paulo (Ferreira) and Willie either side, neither who got forward that much, and with Maka in front, to break through those players would be hard for anyone."

Chelsea won the title at Bolton Wanderers and Terry was presented with it the following week at home to Charlton. "My best days at Chelsea! We'd won the Malaysia Cup in a pre-season and that was the first trophy I lifted. All jokes aside, to people reading this book it probably means nothing, but we still talk about it and see that as the beginning. Then we won the Carling Cup, and we had a confidence about us. When you saw Lamps go through to score at Bolton it was like watching slow motion. Then there was celebrating in front of the fans, Roman coming out, in the dressing room, on top of the bus with the fans..."

The PFA Player of the Year award was special. "I think I was only the third defender ever to win the trophy." He was the first for twelve years. "Even now, when I polish the trophy – I take pride in doing that – it feels such a great achievement for a defender. I know in my heart I'll never win that trophy again, but it means so much to me that all the players who played against us voted for me rather than for strikers."

Mind you, he did score eight goals that season, including the famous winner at home to Barcelona in what many people regard as the greatest game seen at Stamford Bridge.

His hunger for more success was insatiable. "I used to assess things with my dad, and he said 'when can you go for this? Or this?'"

Following the second Champions League semi-final defeat, this time against Liverpool, Chelsea drew there in the Group stage of the following season. The next weekend, in the League, they returned to Anfield and won 4-1. At the end, Terry ordered a team huddle in the centre of the pitch. The remaining Liverpool fans booed furiously. He was determined Chelsea were to make a statement. "When you know the opposition fans hate you, you want to let them know who's won. So we said let's all stay in a huddle. That picture is on the wall in Barney's office (club secretary, David Barnard)."

The trophies came, one after another, mixed in with the heartache of more semi-final defeats, but you're going to get those when your trophy haul keeps building. In 2007 he became the first England player to score at the new Wembley, and the first club captain to raise the FA Cup there. That completed his domestic haul.

"The year before, like every team we were trying to emphasise the importance of the FA Cup in its first year back at Wembley, but we lost the semi-final to Liverpool at Old Trafford, and then Wembley turned out not to be ready. The following season we had our bit of luck and realised it was going to be our year. To walk up those steps, which is an awful long way up by the way, I'll always look back on that."

From the moment John Terry became his club's, his country's and one of the world's most respected defenders, he made it clear time and again he wanted to stay on his home territory. He was Chelsea for life. He desired no contractual uncertainties, no 'want-away' headlines, no big-money moves. He wanted to be Chelsea's Paolo Maldini. He'd built his manor and he wanted to enjoy it and defend it.

"From the day I first walked in and had my first training session with Bobby Oz (Bob Orsborn, Academy coach), and things just happened and you knew in yourself, 'yeah, this is where I want to be.' Chelsea's been very loyal to me. The fans have been exceptional from the word go, they were patient with me and realised when I was young that I needed experience, and when I had the court case they never stopped singing 'Terry for England', they lived through it all with me.

"I'm still close to people from my youth-team days, Nicho, Ozzy." They were both at his wedding along with his youth-team coach Ted Dale. Paul Nicholls was one of three best men with agent and former kitman Aaron Lincoln, and brother Paul. "I still speak to Jon Harley, Mark Hook who was in my youth team. That's how it is. I love Chelsea Football Club."

Alan Hansen, BBC *Match Of The Day* pundit and winner of three European Cups

"John Terry is one of the greatest near-post defenders in the history of the game."

José Mourinho

"There are three kinds of captain: a players' captain, a manager's captain, and a club captain who does all the official things. Most captains are one or two of these. John Terry is all of them."

It really was a funny old game

Jimmy
Greaves

For anyone old enough to have seen the 17-year-old Jimmy Greaves make his Chelsea debut in the first game of the 1957-58 season at Tottenham Hotspur, he is unarguably in Chelsea's Top Ten players of all time.

Many would claim he is the best. All would say he is the club's greatest goalscorer. As recently as 2003, on a vote on Chelsea's official website, he still came fourth in the club's Greatest Player ranking.

Jimmy doesn't do reunions, not with Chelsea or Tottenham, England or West Ham, and certainly not with Milan, the teams he graced. But he agreed to be interviewed for this book. He is still chirpy Jim. He loved his football, but now it is over he doesn't see the need to dwell on it. Yet he was relaxed to talk about his times on one more occasion.

He still does after-dinner speaking, often with Ron 'Chopper' Harris. The natural genius and the bullying hard man! They make a funny pair.

Jimmy, in the comfort of his Chelmsford home, the Essex boy still living in Essex, mused: "You've got to have Chopper and Catty in your top ton. And what about Ruud Gullit?" He likes Ruud Gullit. "He was a great player."

Ruud Gullit changed Chelsea, I suggested. Did Jimmy change Chelsea?

He chuckled. "I don't think I changed anything at Chelsea. If

I did anything at all, I probably kept them in the First Division. I remember when I left they went down!"

Frank Blunstone tells a great story about the genius Jimmy Greaves. Frank was the wonderful left-winger signed from Crewe Alexandra in 1952, who won the League in 1955 and went on to make 347 appearances for the club before retiring through injury in 1964.

"He was an apprentice," Frank recalls. "They used to train at Hendon, the Welsh Harp. They didn't train with us, we didn't know them. We never saw them.

"Every Tuesday, the manager's training programme was First Team versus Reserves, a practice match. This particular Tuesday, we'd had a few injuries on the Saturday, and (manager) Ted Drake sent for two kids to come from Hendon to play in the reserves.

"We started playing, we'd been playing about 20 minutes, and all of a sudden this little kid picks the ball up and sets off on a run. He goes past one, dribbling, no problem, goes past another, and all of a sudden Albert Tennant who was the coach on the touchline, he had one of those megaphones. 'Get rid of it, Jimmy!'

"He goes past another...'For Christ's sake get rid of it, Jimmy!'

"He goes on past another, the goalie comes out, he dips his shoulder and rolls it in the far corner. And that goalie was Reg Matthews, an international! It was absolutely unbelievable!

"He jogged back to the halfway line, gets back there, turns round to the coach and says: 'Albert, you didn't tell me when!'

"Us old pros all thought, 'who the hell is that?' But it was just his sense of humour. He was fantastic."

Jimmy tells the same story in his excellent autobiography *Greavesie*, but he sets it later at a pre-season Blues v Whites match at Stamford Bridge in front of a crowd, and the shouting man on the sideline is Drake himself.

When faced now with choosing between the two stories as to which is most correct, he is uninterested. "It's the same thing", he laughs, "a practice match. I always thought it was Ted, but maybe it was Albert."

All that kerfuffle anyway over what a natural-born goalscorer should do with the ball wasn't his kind of thing. He just enjoyed himself and did the best he could.

"It's always been a belief," he says. "In later years I became good friends with George Best. We used to talk about it. He was another who couldn't really understand all the bollocks going on, managers influencing tactics. You can either play the game or you can't. If you need someone shouting at you from the touchline, you shouldn't be there!"

He played, he scored, he moved on to the next things in life. He doesn't remember the copious goals in any detail.

"The only ones I remember are the ones I've seen on television, and they tended not to be Chelsea goals."

The man who played with a smile famously went on to become a television pundit putting smiles on viewers' faces with his old Liverpool and Scotland opponent Ian St. John during the 1980s. Their excellent Saturday lunchtime show *On The Ball* was a real counter to BBC's *Football Focus*. Somewhere down the line, Jimmy was associated with a catchphrase: 'Funny old game.'

In fact, it was first muttered to him by his *Spitting Images* puppet at the end of a sketch between them. The puppet closed the sketch by looking to the camera and saying it. Brilliantly, if coincidentally, it summed up Jimmy's attitude to football. The puppet's voice, the improvisation, the definition of Jimmy Greaves, man and footballer, had been provided by Harry Enfield.

Jimmy Greaves spent only four seasons in Chelsea's first

team. In the summer of 1961, aged 21, he left. But in those four years he scored 132 goals in 169 games for the club. He was the youngest player ever to reach 100 League goals. He hit 16 England goals in only 15 internationals in his last two years.

By that time his first England captain, Billy Wright, thought he was as good as anyone on the globe.

'No-one can deny that Jimmy Greaves, the 21-year-old Chelsea and England inside-right, has become the most discussed soccerman in the world,' wrote Billy in his *Book Of Soccer* annual.

'Jimmy, who with 41 goals finished on top of the First Division list of goalscorers, thinks and acts so quickly he senses openings few other players dream exist. And it is this co-ordination of thought and movement which has made him the most consistent goalscorer of his generation.'

Yet this skinny, speedy, sinewy slip of a lad, all smiles and optimism, wasn't enormously confident when he joined Chelsea as a 16-year-old. He was aware that David Cliss, joining on the same day, had upstaged him in a London Schoolboys game at White Hart Lane.

Chelsea's famous scout Jimmy Thompson had recruited both, and Jimmy thought Cliss was the man for the future. Also joining on the same day was Ken Shellito, later right-back for both Chelsea and England, and later still manager of Chelsea. These days Ken lives in Malaysia.

"David had a good schoolboy career," he explains, "and everybody was chasing him, and we all thought the same. But it didn't happen for him."

It didn't take long for Jimmy to stamp his superior potential. "About five minutes," Ken laughs. "I'd played against Jimmy when he'd played for Dagenham and I'd played for Romford and Hornchurch.

"He had superb balance. He scored over 100 goals in one

season for the youth team. I think he was the greatest goalscorer England has ever produced."

In fact, he scored 122 goals in that first full season in the youth side. On the Monday after one game when he had netted seven, Ted Drake turned up at the youth-team training ground. Drake reminded Jimmy that he had once scored seven goals himself for Arsenal in a first-team game.

Jimmy recalls the manager saying: "Scoring seven goals in a game happens for a very, very select few, and it happens just once in a lifetime."

He took up the story in his autobiography. 'He placed a hand on my shoulder. "Cherish the memory, son," he told me. "Cherish it forever. That day will never come again."

'In our next game, against Fulham, I scored eight.'

Life as an apprentice, however, wasn't all easy. There were many chores to be done. Believe it or not, he was one of several youngsters who helped erect the first floodlights at Stamford Bridge.

Shellito remembers: "We were working as groundstaff, washing goal nets for a first-team game. It was freezing cold. They were jogging around the pitch, training. He said: 'Ken, I'm going to get into the first team. I can't take much more of this. I want to play.' And not long later Mr Drake put him in at Tottenham and he scored."

Like Peter Bonetti, Jimmy was to play mostly all youth-team football and just two reserve games before making his first-team debut.

But the circumstances of Greaves' debut were unique. It didn't come because of injuries, illnesses or suspensions to others. It didn't come because it was a meaningless end-of-season game. It came on pure selection on the first day of the season away to major rivals Tottenham.

He was marked by the legendary Danny Blanchflower. There is a famous photo from that debut of Greaves weaving through the Tottenham defence with Maurice Norman being one of two defenders watching from their backsides. It was a moment which established him in the minds of the British public. '...who was not impressed by the second-half dribble which took him gliding past three challenges in six yards?' asked one newspaper.

Tottenham scored. Greaves equalised. He remembers that goal. "I could have wished for an easier debut but I kept working and during the second half that graft paid off. I managed to escape from the shackles of Danny for a few brief seconds but that was all the time I needed. When the ball was played through to me I took full advantage of the space I'd created and headed for the Spurs goal. The Spurs keeper Ron Reynolds came off his line, but I saw a gap and planted the ball in."

Jimmy Greaves was up and running. He scored four goals in his first three games.

Peter Brabrook was a team-mate, a fellow Essex boy, one year older, and was to be an England U23 team-mate. They became close friends. He played outside-right. Like Jimmy, he doesn't recall individual goals amongst the 132, apart from in his final game. What he recalls better is the style.

"He had wonderful balance, great skills inside the opponents' box, he hardly missed anything. He was just a natural goalscorer. He just put the ball in the back of the net. He was the greatest goalscorer ever. He never grafted, he never worked, he didn't get back. He just scored goals."

Legend has it that Jimmy's goals were all 'right place at the right time' tap-ins. There were certainly a large number of those. But there was far more to his game than that.

"He went past four or five people as though they weren't there," Peter says. "He very rarely picked the ball up in his own half, more often between the halfway line and the opposition penalty area. And he just went 'zzzsshlump' past two or three. He was so quick over 20 or 30 yards from nothing. They all used to try and kick him, but he had just terrific balance, he did get caught but never seemed to go to ground.

"So I don't know about his best. He scored so many – and I made three-quarters of them!"

The physical attempts to stop the youngster were far more brutal than anything which would be allowed in today's game. Jimmy wasn't bothered. He laughs at it now. Well, he laughs at everything.

"I do quite a lot of theatre work with Chopper now, and he would never stay on the field today if he were playing. But every team had a couple of Choppers. It was just much more physical. There was no particular protection for us, no-one wanted it and no-one asked for it.

"Nowadays people say, look at Billy Wright, he never got booked. But no-one ever got booked. You didn't get booked in those days. There were very few penalties. I took penalties for England from 1959 to 1967, and I never scored a penalty for England! I never scored because I never took one! In the whole time I was the penalty taker, we never got one. That must have been about 50 of my 57 games. Unless there was a deliberate handball, you didn't get a penalty."

In his second game, Chelsea lost 3-2 at home to Manchester City and he and Les Allen scored. In his third, again at Stamford Bridge, Chelsea beat Birmingham City 5-1. He got two, Brabrook one, Allen one and left-winger Jim Lewis scored.

Chris Gibbons started following Chelsea in 1945 as a young boy. By the time of 1955 he was following the team everywhere. He remembers that Birmingham game for a Greaves special goal.

"He picked up the ball in front of the old East Stand, about halfway inside our own half. He went past four defenders, or maybe five, got to the edge of the area and Gil Merrick was the England goalkeeper at the time, and he hammered it past him. You thought he was going to take it up to him and round him like he usually did, but this was Jimmy, always doing the unexpected. He saw Gil Merrick starting to come and he just hammered it."

Jimmy kept scoring. So did the centre-forward next to him, big Ron Tindall, with whom he quickly built up a successful partnership. After eight games he was called up by England U23s. He scored after eight minutes for them. He scored again and then missed a penalty. He always scored on his debuts.

He scored on his Chelsea youth, reserve and first-team debuts, on his Milan, Tottenham and West Ham debuts, on his England U23 and England debuts, and in his first FA Cup Final and European final.

Ted Drake pulled him out of the firing line for six weeks before Christmas to keep his feet on the ground and brought him back for Christmas Day's home game with Portsmouth. He celebrated his return by banging in four in a 7-4 victory. It was his first hat-trick. Senior player Peter Sillett told him: "Four goals after a six-week lay-off? Just think how many you might have scored if you'd been match fit!"

But Chelsea lost the return League fixture the next day 3-0, and drew the following League game, at home to Everton, 3-3. They conceded too many goals.

In mid-February he struck another hat-trick, all the goals in a 3-2 win against Sheffield Wednesday at Hillsborough, but by then the harsh realities of life at the top had been stamped on him. He was left out of an FA Cup fourth-round replay at Darlington, not for modern rotation purposes, but because he hadn't played well in the home game and maybe as some protection as he was still young.

Chelsea lost pathetically, 4-1 after extra-time, and having berated each player and left the dressing room Drake returned and shouted: "As for you Greaves, Mr Bloody England U23, some player you are, you can't even get in this side."

Chelsea finished his first season exactly mid-table, 11th. They scored 83 League goals and conceded 79. Greaves was top scorer with 22. That was grand for a youngster, but he was well down the top hot shots' list in the top flight:

Tommy Thompson (Preston) 34, Gordon Turner (Luton) 33, Jimmy Murray (Wolves) 30, Tom Finney (Preston) 26, Joe Hayes (Manchester City) 25, David Herd (Arsenal) 24, Bobby Robson (West Bromwich Albion) 24, Norman Deeley (Wolves) 23, Ronnie Allen (West Bromwich Albion) and Jimmy 22.

Finney, of course, was a winger. Robson, Sir Bobby, was a wing-half.

Jimmy readily admits it was a different world. He wasn't concerned Chelsea weren't winning things or challenging for trophies. In 53 years the club had won one trophy.

"I didn't think we were crap," he said. "Well, I did, but I was happy playing in a crap team and was with a great bunch of lads. It was fabulous. The Sillett brothers! I adored Peter, and John's still one of my great pals, I've known him since I was 15. Peter Brabrook, Frank Blunstone. We lost a dear friend a few months ago, Tony Nicholas.

"Derek Saunders was someone I looked up to when I joined. Ron Tindall was a great laugh, a great guy to be with. I knew no better, I loved it."

And people loved being with him. Ken Shellito was one. "When we became professionals, we'd train, then he'd say 'let's go up to town,' and we'd go up to the cartoon cinema in the afternoon and watch cartoons. He absolutely loved them."

Peter Brabrook was enjoying his company as well. "He wasn't one for the limelight. He was just a natural goalscorer and a great lad. Him, the Silletts. There was nothing nasty. He was just a really, really nice guy."

But the trouble was Chelsea had been champions in 1955, and had lost the heart of that side. Roy Bentley, Eric Parsons and Stan Willemse had moved on, Stan Wicks had played his last game because of injury and Bobby Smith and Les Allen were now moving on to Tottenham to form the front partnership that would win the first League and Cup double of the century.

Chelsea's signing policy was also poor. Joe Baker, later an England centre-forward, was released and Dave Mackay, later the heart of the Tottenham double team, was rejected when a purchase was available from Hearts in favour of Sylvan Anderton from Reading. Anderton didn't flourish.

On a Saturday matchday, Jimmy would be picked up by Brabrook and the Sillett brothers, and their purchased pre-match meal at a café would be roast beef, Yorkshire pudding plus trimmings, or pie and mash followed by blackcurrant crumble and custard.

Jimmy married during his first season, and he and his wife Irene had their first child in his second. They moved into a flat that was on the Plough Lane premises of Wimbledon Football Club, then non-League. Later, Chelsea helped them move back to Essex.

It is impossible to measure just how different the world was. "I received no coaching as such other than the odd tips from Albert Tennant and senior pros. My real football education took place out on the pitch during actual games. I'd try something in a game and if it didn't work, I'd try something else."

In his second season, 1958-59, kicking off when he was just 18, he scored 32 League goals. He was the equal top scorer, the Golden Boot as it would be now, with Tottenham's Bobby Smith. It set a new club record, beating the 30 Bob Whittingham scored in Division Two in 1910-11. Chelsea's

top-flight record had been 26 by Tommy Lawton in 1946-47. He received an illuminated address from the club for this, his second such address. They had given him one for his season in the juniors.

This time Jimmy had scored eight goals in his first three games. The third match was remarkable. It was against Wolves, who boasted England's half-back line of Bill Slater, Billy Wright and Ron Flowers. Jimmy scored five.

'There were certain games when I took to the pitch and just knew I was going to have one of those games when everything would go my way,' he writes in his autobiography. 'From my first touch of the ball I felt comfortable. In our first real attack, I corkscrewed past Ron Flowers and (left-back) Gerry Harris before playing a one-two with Peter Brabrook. Though shackled by Bill Slater I'd seen a gap just to the left of (goalkeeper) Malcolm Finlayson and aimed for that.

'Whenever I was presented with such an opportunity, I never hit the ball with all the power I could muster because I didn't have to. When I saw an opening I would simply "pass" the ball through the space knowing no-one could reach it. Most of the goals I scored were like that.

'Rarely did I hit a spectacular shot from 30 yards. It was all about ghosting into space and hoping a team-mate had spotted me on the run and would thread through a well-weighted pass. If not that, then I attacked the ball. I was a predator of the penalty box who made space to score goals. I'd pass the ball, stroke it, side-foot it, chip it or drive it into the net depending on the situation.'

Frank Blunstone, whose opportunities to line up with Jimmy were restricted by injury and national service, recalls: "I played with Jimmy for two years, and when you play with people you get to know everything about them. Now, I could never work Jimmy out. I never knew whether he was left-footed or right-footed. That's how good he was.

"He could take them either way. If you put him in on his right he'd do it, if you put him in on his left he'd do it. I couldn't tell. Many was the time I thought are you left-footed or right-footed?"

In the remainder of the season he got another hat-trick at home to Nottingham Forest, and two more goals as well in the FA Cup plus three in Chelsea's opening European campaign, the Inter-Cities Fairs Cup. But Chelsea went out of the FA Cup in the fourth round, at home to Aston Villa, out in the second round in Europe, and finished 14th in the First Division, scoring 77 and conceding 98.

Ken Shellito didn't see just a goalscorer and nothing else emerging. "He was better for the team than 10 men plus 35 goals a season," Ken says. Already some newspapers were questioning his work rate. "He was unique.

"People who score goals, look at (Alan) Shearer recently, Pelé, Eusebio, Bobby Charlton...I look at Jimmy, I know it was earlier and defences were not so educated, but people still used their ability to score. Jimmy had it.

"How many times did Jimmy hit a powerful shot into goal? He never did. He glided it in. He had balance!"

At the end of his second season, he finally made it into the England team. By now he was 19. Remarkably, Brabrook had made it in at a younger age. But Brabrook was to get stuck on three caps. Greaves went on to win 57.

With England he teamed up with Blackpool's right-back Jimmy Armfield, later a long-serving commentator on BBC Radio Five Live. Armfield once said: "Jimmy Greaves was unique because he was the same player at 18 as he was at 28." The goalscorer!

Jimmy likes that. "Jim and I cut our back teeth together in international football. We were together before Bobby Moore came on the scene for England U23s and on tour. We were both young men and at the same time finding our feet and have remained great friends ever since. I recall Jim and I as very, very raw young boys."

A player of his skill and speed in a team which was scoring so many goals, even in addition to his own, was obviously setting up his fair share of assists too. For a start, there were those wicked inswinging corners from the right flank when he wasn't in the penalty area to finish.

It seems that at the ripe, advanced age of 67, he hasn't thought of himself ever as a maker of goals.

"I assume so," he said in consideration when asked about his creativity for others. It was, for him, quite careful consideration of a facet of his career. "I think so. I'd like to think that throughout my career, but this is sometimes overlooked. There was actually a period at Tottenham of about two or three years when I took corners from the left and right."

In his third Chelsea season, he was 19, he scored 29 League goals and one in the FA Cup. He got a hat-trick on the opening day in a 4-4 draw at home to Preston North End. He got another hat-trick in September in a 4-2 home win over Birmingham. And in December he scored five for a second time in a famous 5-4 victory at Preston.

This was the game when each time he scored, Preston equalised. 0-1, 1-1; 1-2, 2-2; 2-3, 3-3; 3-4, 4-4. John Sillett was right-back and Peter Sillett left-back. After the fourth equaliser, John approached his friend.

"John came up and said the big fella (Peter) says we're all in for a bollocking if we lose this having scored four goals away from home. The big fella says for Christ's sake put one in the back of the net. And he promised they wouldn't let another in. So I asked: 'Do I have any guarantees?' 'He promised', he said. 'But you've already let in four', I said. That's how it was. It was a happy team." Of course, he supplied the fifth.

But despite his goals, the team was struggling more and more. Shellito recalls one match up north which resulted in a 2-0 defeat.

"Everyone got back in the dressing room and sat about in silence. Mr Drake came in to speak to us, looked around and said: 'Where's Jimmy?' Jimmy shouted: 'I'm in the bath, boss.' Mr Drake called: 'What are you doing in the bath?' And Jimmy replied: 'It's bleedin' cold out there boss, I've been waiting 90 minutes to come in and get warm!'"

Jimmy refutes, however, that he didn't take the game seriously. He admits he hated the long distance running in training, but says he worked hard on his speed and sharpness.

By now he was the most glamorous player in the country. The top youngsters were Bobby Charlton at Manchester United, Johnny Haynes at Fulham and Jimmy. Jimmy even accepted the offer of an agent, who found him work outside football. He did a *Bovril* advertisement which appeared on the back of all Wembley programmes at internationals and Cup Finals for a long time.

But this was the period when question marks about his future began to develop in his mind. Chelsea got to April and were in a relegation battle. Once again, elimination from the FA Cup had been at home to Aston Villa in the fourth round – that had been two years running by the same team, same round, same venue, same score: 1-2.

Youngsters like Cliss, Mel Scott and Johnny Brooks, all of whom joined on the same day as Jimmy, and new signing Charlie Livesey, had failed to shine in the first team. In the end Chelsea finished two places above relegation, scoring 76 goals and conceding 91.

But April had brought three wins, including away at Arsenal and Tottenham, and he approached his fourth season with renewed optimism.

Jimmy Greaves' fourth and final season with Chelsea is probably the greatest individual season by a Chelsea player. He scored 41 League goals in 40 games, and a further two in the new League Cup competition on his debut in it.

Amazingly, he didn't score in his first two matches. But before August was out he hit a hat-trick in a 3-3 home draw with Wolves. In September he scored a treble in a 5-2 home win over Blackburn. In November he claimed another hat-trick in a 6-3 home win over Manchester City. In December he scored five for a third time in a 7-1 home win over West Bromwich Albion. In March he knocked in four in a 6-1 away win at Newcastle. And in his last game for the club, the last game of the season, when his move to Milan had been announced, he captained Chelsea for the first time and scored all four goals in a 4-3 victory over Nottingham Forest before the crowd surged onto the pitch and lifted him shoulder high to carry him round on a lap of honour.

Chelsea scored 98 League goals in that 1960-61 season – and conceded 100. The team finished 12th. Fourth Division Crewe won 2-1 in the FA Cup third round at Stamford Bridge. League defeats included 4-1 at Bolton (Jimmy scored), 6-2 at home to Burnley (Jimmy scored one), 6-0 at Manchester United, 6-1 next game at Wolves (the Crewe defeat was next), and 3-0 at West Brom.

Jimmy had his own personal tragedy during the season when his and Irene's second child, Jimmy Jr, died aged four months from pneumonia. Shellito remembers the scene sadly. "We went to the funeral and he brought his England shirt there, and then Jimmy tried to jump in as the coffin was lowered down. It was very sad. He has had a hard life."

Two financial issues were emerging. Firstly, in England, there was still a salary cap on professional footballers, standing at £20 a week. There wasn't in Italy, and the restriction on foreign players being imported to Italy was being lifted for the following season. Italian clubs were seeking English forwards.

Secondly, Chelsea's finances were unhealthy. When Greaves told the board of his restlessness, they told him of Milan's interest. A deal was done. The transfer fee would be a massive £80,000 with £10,000 of that up front.

At first, Jimmy agreed to move and sign. But then he had second thoughts. The Professional Footballers' Association was winning its battle with the FA to remove the salary cap in England and there was talk of Johnny Haynes being paid £100 a week. Jimmy was a home boy. He wanted to live in Essex. He wanted to play for Chelsea.

He tried to get out of the move. "I didn't want to leave!" he says with certainty now. "Milan came in for me, Chelsea wanted me to go, and at first I thought I may just as well give it a try. But, after the reality set in, I dearly wanted to stay.

"I told the club and they said they'd try to get me out of it. They gave me a solicitor, but all he did was get me a pay rise from Milan. At no time at all was it Chelsea's intention to get me out of it. It's sad."

Things got worse. Chelsea insisted he went on an end-of-season tour. He refused. They suspended him and he missed a couple of England internationals.

The Greaves era was over. Amazingly, Bobby Tambling emerged from the youth and reserves to score even more goals, albeit over a longer period. But Chelsea were relegated next season, coming bottom. They scored a measly 63 goals and conceded a traditional 94. David Cliss was sold to Brentford.

At Milan, Jimmy scored nine goals in 12 games in the most defensive league in the world, possibly in history, but never settled. He wanted home. When Milan made him available midway through the season, Chelsea had first option to buy him back, but failed to match Tottenham's money. Tottenham had just won the League and Cup double. Chelsea were heading for relegation. It was an easy choice for him.

At Tottenham he scored a hat-trick on his debut, was top scorer in a season eight times, and won the FA Cup twice and the European Cup Winners' Cup, the first time an English side won a European trophy. He would surely be in their Top Ten players ever.

For England he finished with an incredible 44 goals in 57 games. Record scorer Bobby Charlton scored his 49 in 106 matches, Gary Lineker took 80 games to score his 48 goals. Michael Owen finished the calendar year 2007 as fourth top England scorer with 40 goals from 88 games. There has been no-one like Jimmy Greaves.

Headlines continued to follow him. In 1966 he was left out of the England World Cup final team following injury. In the 1970s he admitted to alcoholism. But none of this was the Jimmy Greaves of Chelsea. The Jimmy of Chelsea was simply the greatest goalscorer in the history of the universe.

Jimmy never did well against Chelsea for Tottenham or West Ham. True, he won the FA Cup Final in 1967 against his old club, but didn't score much, just four in 19 games. Having retired in 1971, he returned to Stamford Bridge on April 21st 1980 to participate in Ron Harris's second testimonial.

"Chopper" was coming up to 20 years at the club and was moving on. He put together a Past XI to play the current team. The current team was in the doldrums. Guess what happened! Chelsea 0 Chelsea Past XI 1. Guess who scored! Forty-year-old Jimmy Greaves.

"I remember that!" he chuckles. "I played a one-two with, I think it was Frank Stapleton who was playing centre-forward." No, Jim. It kicked off with Peter Osgood and Ian Hutchinson up front, who were replaced by Bobby Tambling and Bill Garner. You came on for Ray Wilkins.

"Ian Botham played, I remember that." Correct. And you got through in the last minute and hammered the ball into the roof of the net at the Shed End. "That's right! Isn't it amazing how you remember things like that and not the other goals!"

You get the feeling with Jimmy Greaves that he is where he wants to be. Having been divorced by his teenage bride Irene during the depths of alcoholism, they were separated for all of three months afterwards before he faced up to his demons, stopped drinking, and they have been back together ever since. Their grandchildren number double figures.

He may not appear regularly on television anymore, but he can afford to choose his after-dinner appearances to suit himself, and he has written a weekly column in *The Sun* for nearly 20 years. He may not like reunions, but he follows his old clubs, and has visited Chelsea quietly and without fuss to see the odd game.

He has his views on football, still coloured by the glory of scoring goals. They include views on modern-day Chelsea.

"A couple of years ago, I'm going to blow my own trumpet here, when Drogba wasn't the Blue Boy of Chelsea, I said I'd love to play next to him. When he first came in the side there were a lot of question marks about him. He kept falling over, his ball control wasn't all it should be, and a lot of people were doubting him. I said I thought he was a good player.

"He needed someone to get hold of him, tell him to stop mucking about, stop falling over, and to concentrate on his game. I said he was not only a good player, he was the sort of player who would help you to play better.

"I'm so pleased for him that he's got it right now. Tell him he's our family hero. My grandson loves him."

Jim, you are still a hero to thousands of Chelsea families. I'm sure you know, but I wonder if you appreciate to what degree. If I could change one thing in your life, it would be to let you be loved by them now. It would mean a lot to thousands of people, and it would then surely mean a lot to you. If you gave them that opportunity, the power of the old feelings would astonish you.

But, more importantly, it is so good that one of the happiest as well as one of the greatest players ever to pull on a Chelsea shirt, is so happy again.

Ken Shellito on what Jimmy Greaves the player might be like now

"Jim was Jim! I don't think he would have adapted to different systems. He was a kid who grew up to live and thrive on his ability. The attitude today doesn't encourage the likes of Jimmy in case the manager loses his job. But I think he would save jobs!"

Peter Brabrook on what Jimmy Greaves the player might be like now

"Without a doubt he'd adapt. He'd have the sharpness in and around the box. He'd be like a Michael Owen, similar size, very quick, not a great contribution to the team or great work rate, but he'd score goals for fun. Michael Owen survives. Jimmy would. He was full of confidence on and off the field."

Ken Shellito on that last game against Nottingham Forest

"It was his best game, against Nottingham Forest. He said to me, 'Ken, I'm going to go out with a hat-trick.' He scored all four. It was 4-3. They carried him off the field. I look back and it was an absolutely superb day. That's the way he was!"

Peter Brabrook on that last game
against Nottingham Forest

"We played Nottingham Forest at home, the last game he played before he went to Italy, we won 4-3 and he got all four goals. One was a penalty, and each one, even the penalty, he mis-kicked, but they all went in. He went for a header and it hit his shins, he went for a side-foot but it hit his knee. That kind of thing! I'm not sure any of the goals hit the back of the net, but they all crossed the line. That was Jimmy. He did it from youth age to international level! Goals! It was just so easy! That was Greavesie."

Most hat-tricks for Chelsea

13 in 169 games, Jimmy Greaves, 1957-1961;
10 in 164 games, George Hilsdon (including two for one six-goal performance), 1906-1912;
8 in 420 games, Kerry Dixon, 1983-1992;
8 in 370 games, Bobby Tambling, 1958-1970.

It wasn't all crazy at all – not quite

Dennis Wise

Dennis Wise was man of the match on his Chelsea debut, playing like an old fashioned right-winger and destroying Derby County left-back Michael Forsyth. He put over cross after cross for Kerry Dixon. Chelsea won 2-1. In his second game he was sent off after ten minutes along with Crystal Palace's Andy Gray for fighting. Crazy days!

There were eleven years of that.

He struggled to adapt at first following his £1.6m move from Wimbledon in 1990, yet he quickly built up an extraordinary relationship with the fans that was full of humour and two-way communication even during the game. He became the cult successor to the likes of David Webb and Joey Jones.

"That's one thing I did do," he says with pleasure. "I think I just wanted them to enjoy themselves more than anything. I remember one situation when someone got injured and I had a game of head-tennis with one of the punters, and it was fun. They made it fun, they made me enjoy it."

Chelsea were in the process of beating Leicester City 4-0 at the time in 1994. He'd become captain by then. Arguably, there had been no less obvious a candidate for captain in his early years. Arguably, he became Chelsea's best captain until the emergence of John Terry. He was the best and the most successful of the first 100 years.

Typically, he set a trend on the Lap of Appreciation following the final home game of each season, and then on laps of honour as his Chelsea became serial winners, of taking a child out of the crowd and including them on each lap.

"When I was a young lad", he explains, "training with my dad's team, I remember Stan Bowles coming over. He was my hero when I was a kid. He knew my dad, and he spent, five, ten minutes with me showing me ball skills. Just to have time with him, being the only one with him, was very nice. I used to do that all the time."

Stan Bowles, Queens Park Rangers legend! The man who famously lost a fortune with his betting!

Early in Wise's second season at Chelsea, in stoppage time at QPR, the team was 2-1 down. Vinnie Jones took a long throw, Ken Monkou headed it on and Wise executed a wonderful overhead kick to claim a dramatic and outstanding equaliser.

He remembers the goal more than anything now for his hero. "I lost Stan Bowles a load of money," he laughs out loud. "He was booing me. He was sitting in a box with my dad and he went potty!" He laughs some more. Dennis Wise is still enjoying himself.

Wise was sent off nine times in his Chelsea career. One season, 1998-99, he was sent off four times including once in pre-season for which he received a three-game ban in the Premiership. That had been when the team was losing 4-0 to a Juninho-inspired Atletico Madrid, and he just hated losing. Bad tackle! Red card!

The second incident occurred in the final minutes of a 4-1 League Cup win over Aston Villa. He'd lost the ball, he lost his mind. Two-footed tackle on Darren Byfield. Red card. Four-match ban!

Half-an-hour later he was sitting perplexed in the Players' Bar. "That wasn't a sending off, was it?" he enquired indignantly when I walked in.

"Yes!" I replied. "It was a two-footed tackle!"

He shook his head in disbelief. It was clear what he was thinking. He'd lost the ball, what did anyone expect him to do? The fact that it was 4-1 and wasteful action was an irrelevance.

In between those incidents, in the first game of the Premiership season when highly-fancied Chelsea were stupidly losing 2-1 at Coventry City, he got booked for dissent. Chelsea had a free-kick, and Wise demanded the defensive wall go back to his version of ten yards. The referee's version was different. So Wise furiously marched out the ten strides himself, and was carded for dissent.

Later that evening in a London street, he insistently told his wife-to-be Claire that he knew exactly what ten yards was, and finished up pacing the precise distance out for her.

There were no issues on which Wise could bear losing. Maybe that's how he became Chelsea's outstanding leader and winner of the club's first century.

In his tenth season at Chelsea, when he was going to lift the FA Cup and be voted Player of the Year, both for the second time, Dennis Wise participated in the Champions League, Chelsea's first time in the competition.

On Matchday Five, they needed a result away to Milan, in the San Siro, to establish a group position above the Italians going into the final game. Chelsea dominated, then Milan scored against the run of play with just over sixteen minutes left. Three minutes later, Dennis Wise equalised.

"It was a fantastic ball from Robbie Di Matteo, and Maldini was asleep for a minute. You can't really leave me to creep in behind you!"

It wasn't only Paolo Maldini whom Wise defeated with his run, but Roberto Ayala also, two of the finest defenders in

Europe. He pulled Di Matteo's chip down with the top of his right foot as it came from over his shoulder, and then he planted the ball between the legs of the advancing goalkeeper Abbiati with his left. It was a magical moment and it was sublime technique. Chelsea went on to win the group.

Wise peeled off to the left in celebration, realised the Chelsea fans were to the right and changed direction to celebrate with them.

"What I loved about that goal and didn't realise at the time until I saw it on telly was how the bench celebrated, just how much it meant to them, Luca and everyone jumping up and down, going mad. All of them, it meant so much."

Indeed, Gianluca Vialli and the management team and substitutes did go crazy. Chelsea had gone from a middle-of-the-road team to a top European one, and Wise had led them and been top man when it mattered.

The goal led to a famous Dennis Wise song still repeated by Chelsea fans today. But the details of that – the lyrics – aren't suitable here!

Dennis Wise is the only player in this Top Ten who was a Chelsea record purchase at the time of his signing. But his first season didn't go well.

He had come from a Wimbledon team where he had to receive the ball wide and knock it into the penalty area quickly for physical strikers to do battle. Although Pat Nevin had left Chelsea two summers previously, Wise was signed essentially as a replacement for him. But Nevin used to trick his way to the byline and hang crosses to the far post for Kerry Dixon to outjump defenders. It was very different.

Chelsea were a team in transition, and although the League Cup semi-final was reached, it was a disappointing campaign. At one point, Wise was struggling to retain his place with young widemen Graham Stuart and Graeme Le Saux laying claim to the wings.

But the 23-year-old with the tearaway reputation from his *Crazy Gang* days at Wimbledon had a number of qualities in his locker: a professional attitude to training, a huge ability to learn, two great feet and a range of passing that was to become increasingly recognised. He also possessed a sense of responsibility to his team, and the extraordinary passion to win.

"There were a lot of things I had to learn," he admits now. "Where I came from was very structured, the Harry Bassett way, you all knew what you had to do. I was always one to listen to all that, I was one who could take things on board.

"I used to hate people going home early after training. I always wanted to learn. It wasn't a question of how much you were earning, I wanted to work, I wanted to get on with the work.

"Things have changed a lot over the years and agents don't always help the situation. I was talking to a player about maybe signing when I was Leeds manager, and he said 'how much will you pay?' I thought, 'hang on, how much do you want to come and play for Leeds?'"

Yes, this is Dennis Wise, now executive director (football) at Newcastle United, former manager of Leeds and one-time player-manager of FA Cup finalists Millwall. He remains the fighting-for-victory man.

In his fourth game, his last before suspension following the first sending off, Chelsea were drawing 2-2 with Sunderland and won a late penalty. Dixon had missed one the match before. Wise, comfortable with the responsibility, stepped up and smacked the winner. Almost immediately, he had become team penalty taker.

His spiky attitude was recognised at international level, and he won his first caps that May, scoring England's winner in Turkey on his debut in a European Championship qualifier.

Bobby Campbell had been the manager to buy him. For Wise's second season, Ian Porterfield took over. The football was more direct. His old pal Vinnie Jones was signed. He began to thrive.

But on the way to an FA Cup quarter-final replay defeat and more lack of achievement, something momentous happened. Chelsea went to Liverpool, played a 4-5-1 formation (Wise being used in central midfield for the first time) and won 2-1. It was a real footballing performance, pass and move. Wise scored the winner and it was the team's first victory at Anfield since 1966.

"I had always played in central midfield and I wanted to play there again," he says. "But Dave Bassett had shifted me over to being a winger because Wimbledon played that different way." Dennis had too many touches on the ball in central midfield for Bassett's liking.

"Ian Porterfield used me as an attacking player in a midfield three and it worked well with Vinnie holding, and me and Andy Townsend going forward. Vinnie scored a scorcher, 25 yards, and I was able to get forward and score the winner."

A couple of weeks before he had scored the opening goal in an FA Cup tie at Hull City, and jumped into the crowd. At Anfield, at half-time when it was 1-1, a fan in the toilet at the away end said: "I hope Wisey gets the winner 'cos he'll jump in with us." The cult was already catching on. And that is what happened.

"You just do it," Dennis chuckles. "It's just the passion of it. It's naturalness coming out. That was me. You didn't think about celebrations. But you'd get booked for it now. You didn't then. It's gone crazy!"

He finished his second season as top scorer with fourteen goals. Things were improving, but they were about to get even better.

His favourite coach, Don Howe, was brought in to help

Porterfield and by Christmas of his third season Chelsea were in the top four with Wise playing his best football so far. But Howe suffered a heart scare and Chelsea's young side, still in transition, lost direction, went out of the Cups early and yet again challenged for nothing.

In February, David Webb replaced Porterfield in order to steady the ship, and Wise began to think his future was elsewhere.

"I would probably have left if he had stayed," he admits. "I don't think he liked me as a player. And he wasn't the best man I've worked under. I didn't mind him as a bloke but he was very aggressive about what he wanted to do. That was his judgement and he preferred other people ahead of me. I think I proved him wrong."

In the shake-up, Webb's successful saving of Chelsea didn't get him the job permanently. Glenn Hoddle was introduced to make big changes. Dennis Wise was about to become the biggest change.

Wise had played 122 games and scored 31 goals. Good, but not great. Captain and star Andy Townsend had moved on, and so had young hopefuls Stuart and Le Saux. They were all to win things before Chelsea.

Hoddle and his assistant Peter Shreeves made Wise captain. It was an easy decision and it was a very hard one at the same time. Wise was easily the best player, the only one with a chance of leading the team by quality example.

That was shown in the opening League game against Blackburn when he crossed with the outside of his right foot from an inside-left position for debutant Gavin Peacock to head the team into the lead. Hoddle was playing with just three at the back, and Wise was again in a more central role. But he was only team captain. The management didn't trust him to be club captain with his tearaway attitude.

"Glenn gave it to me, and he took it away from me as well," Dennis says matter-of-factly. "And then he gave it back again. That's what happens when you step out of line."

The taking away happened during his second season under Hoddle. In all, he served him for three years, and they were tempestuous. They also marked Wise out as emerging as a very special player.

Chelsea lost that match to Blackburn, and the re-introduction of the beautiful game didn't start well. By Boxing Day, Chelsea dropped into the relegation zone following a defeat at Southampton. In the dressing room afterwards, Wise was unimpressed by Hoddle's talk, and demanded that it was time for the team to start getting stuck in. A row exploded.

Wise had not been sent off since his first season, but then had suffered his second red card in October at West Ham, and Hoddle had been furious. Now the two were at war in front of the team.

"We had a big argument over a few things," Dennis recalls. "I'm a different person to Glenn. Glenn wants to win as much as I do, but I probably step over the line more than him. I don't care how I win. He didn't agree with the way I did this. A few dummies were spat out, but it became better. After that there was a little more respect for each other."

The facts were that Wise's football had stepped up another gear despite Chelsea's results. Shreeves acted as mediator in the row, and Hoddle changed the shape of the team to four at the back with a midfield diamond, Wise on the left, and it worked. It got steelier, it grew in belief, and Wise became only the third captain in the club's history to lead them out in an FA Cup Final at the end of the season.

He had, of course, won the FA Cup aged 21 with Wimbledon. He so nearly won it again in 1994. But after Peacock had hit the bar and Chelsea had been the better team for the first 55 minutes, everything went wrong and

Manchester United won 4-0. He has never watched a tape of the game. "I really dislike that day. There are certain moments in that game, if onlys, if onlys, but 'if onlys' aren't good enough...I'd rather forget it!"

But for Chelsea fans it was an important milestone. The team hadn't been in an FA Cup Final for 24 years, nor any kind of major final for 22 years. What was more, Manchester United won the League and Cup double, so Chelsea qualified for the European Cup Winners' Cup.

In the first leg of the first round, Wise scored an often forgotten, outstanding goal. Against Viktoria Zizkov in filthy rain at Stamford Bridge, he received the ball just outside his area, hit a marvellous cross-field pass to Paul Furlong, made a great run, got the ball back 35 yards out, used Furlong as a decoy in a non-one-two and stepped inside a defender to smash a left-footer into the top corner.

"That was a good goal and a crucial goal as well," he remembers enthusiastically. "It was about 35 yards. But before I scored, I took a corner and when I took it I slipped and the ball went out for a throw-in where I'd been standing. They'd gone up the other end and I think the television was more interested in re-showing that than the goal."

His form now was consistently international class, and he got back in the England team and was standing out. And for all his run-ins with Hoddle, he was not only benefiting from the style of football, he was learning off the man who had discovered European methods for himself by playing abroad.

"Glenn made me realise a lot of things about looking after yourself. I ate the right things, did the right things at the right time, I worked hard at my football. When you're younger and you get a bit of money, you're naive and think 'let's go and enjoy ourselves' when we should be focusing on what you need to focus on which is football, because that's what's got you where you are."

Hoddle was learning from him too. In the second round in Europe, at home to Austria Memphis, Wise declared at half-time that he thought he could get his man-marker Schmid, who had already been booked, sent off. Hoddle enthusiastically told him to do it. He did – two tackles from behind! Schmid was suspended for the second leg and Chelsea's European adventure progressed.

But just as things were going so well, they crashed. Following the very game when Wise played head-tennis with a West Stand spectator, the 4-0 win over Leicester, a game where he had played so well, he went for a good night out. He got in an argument with a taxi driver, and finished up being charged with assault.

Hoddle withdrew the captaincy from him. Wise was furious with the lack of support. No announcement was made but in the next game, at Arsenal, Peacock led the team out and wore the armband. Typically, belligerent Wise gave Chelsea the lead. Typically he started the move, taking goalkeeper Kharine's throw in the centre-circle, passing out left to Peacock, and then turning up in the penalty area to score when the resulting cross was headed back. And typically Chelsea lost 3-1.

Wise is a little more mellowed about Hoddle's conduct now. "It was a learning process at the time. I loved being captain. He could have fined me, but he knew if he took it away it would hurt me more than anything."

The truth is it hurt Chelsea, too. Peacock was a good man, but Wise knew the name of every reserve and youth-team player, he was beginning to dig people out when they weren't pulling their weight, he was determined to drag his side to silverware and his leadership was missed.

"I was a principled kind of person," he insists. "There were certain standards that you want. Everyone goes by the book and no-one takes any liberties. No-one is different from anyone else."

Worse still, he suffered a bad thigh injury which required surgery, and he had to face the court case over the taxi incident when not playing. It affected him badly. He missed the last three months of the season, but he won his case and got his precious armband back.

Chelsea went out of Europe in the semi-final, and after two seasons of increasing achievement, now faced a new one without anything special to look forward to.

"It was very frustrating. We were so close sometimes. But at the time we weren't good enough and knew it. We needed extra.

"Bringing in Ruud and Mark Hughes was the extra! Then players who could play at that level stayed, and those who couldn't got knocked aside."

That summer, when Ruud Gullit was holding a press conference about his arrival and the signing of Mark Hughes was announced, Wise was training alone in order to recover from his operation. There was no fear about his position. He told me at the time: "Do yourself a favour and put some money on us to win something now."

He confirms he didn't feel threatened. "When you want to win things, you need the best players, and we were getting the best players. It's up to you to fight for that place, and if you fight, then you play if you play well. That's what football's all about. It's not about spitting your dummy out and saying 'why have you bought him, have you bought him to replace me?' You have to stand your ground."

In fact, the 1995-96 season was a tough one for him, trying to find his rhythm after the injury. But Gullit saw a leader, a commitment and an attitude that he liked. Chelsea were playing three at the back once more, Wise was in a central role again, and he was relishing the involvement.

He continued to be the hub of the side – when he couldn't play, the team couldn't perform – and as his rhythm returned, so did his form. He scored a wonderful, top-corner 35-yarder at Southampton and typically went charging up the pitch to celebrate with goalkeeper Kevin Hitchcock because no-one ever celebrated with him. Halfway towards him he changed his mind because it was too far, and so celebrated on his own.

Just before Christmas Gullit was moved to midfield, and off his own bat Wise became more defensive. "I had to change," he says with relish. "There are sacrifices you have to make. It was something I wasn't too worried about doing. It's something players have to do.

"If you get a world-class player, you have to sacrifice yourself to get them on the ball. Ruud could cause havoc! He was unbelievably powerful."

But Wise's influence wasn't reduced. In a game at Queens Park Rangers, in front of the Main Stand, he found himself on the ball faced with three QPR players and Gullit motionless in advance of them. The whole stand heard him shout: "Oi, Ruudi, get your ****ing arse back here." The home fans roared mockingly. Gullit's colour darkened noticeably, but he did what he was told.

Similarly, after a home FA Cup draw with Wimbledon, he spoke out in a team meeting in advance of the replay when Hoddle was preparing tactics. "**** Wimbledon, we're better than them. Let's just go out and beat them!"

Hoddle turned to Gullit for support, saying you had to prepare for teams like Wimbledon. But Gullit supported Wise. Chelsea won a great replay 3-1.

Chelsea played some wonderful football that season, better than anything since the early 1970s, but still went out in the semi-final of the FA Cup and were only 11th in the League. Wise was in the England squad all through the year, but didn't play much.

In the last week of the season, Hoddle was announced as the next England manager. Wise walked into the training ground canteen after hearing and joked: "I'd like to announce my international retirement." In fact, he was left out of the squad by Terry Venables for the European Championships held in England. He went on holiday to avoid them, but still watched every game.

In just over two years as England manager, Hoddle never picked him. It was silly. But in 2000, when Wise was starring in the Champions League, Hoddle told me in a filmed interview that were he still England manager he would definitely pick him now.

Remarkably, Hoddle changed Wise for the better and gave him the chance to move towards being a world-class player. Wise recognises that now. But their ways of going about things couldn't have been more divided.

So in 1996, Gullit became Chelsea manager. Wise was 29-years-old, had won nothing with the club and had been there six years. He had become a superb player, but not yet Top Ten material. He had played 236 games and scored 52 goals. Over the next four years he was to become a true history maker.

"Chelsea was a club that maybe just wanted to stay at a level. And then all of a sudden it wanted to build from there. That's what it did, and the players who turned up: Gianfranco, Ruud, Robbie, Luca, there were so many. Marcel, Le Saux, Leboeuf, Gus Poyet. They were all quality, players with a lot of quality. And they were good people as well. If you haven't got good people, you haven't got a prayer of doing anything or winning anything. It was good that they picked the right players.

"I'd try and help as much as I could, make players welcome. It was quite straightforward, trying to make them enjoy life here and help them as much as possible. I remember Luca when he first came, me and Claire used to take him to the pictures every Friday, and take him for a pizza. It was just a case of making sure everyone was comfortable.

"At first a lot of the Italians couldn't believe how relaxed it was. They enjoyed themselves and it was important they enjoyed it."

And so he taught Roberto Di Matteo to say: "Thank you hairy crotch," instead of "Thank you very much," and he ripped the last two chapters out of an English novel Gianfranco Zola was reading in order to improve his English. Poor Franco couldn't understand the ending – or lack of it. But when he ended a goalscoring drought and sank to his knees, Wise pulled him up, kissed him and told him he'd give him back the chapters. Zola, gentleman that he is, just refrained from murdering him on the pitch there and then!

Wise had always been on set plays. Since coming to the club he took them all. But with the arrival of Frank Leboeuf he surrendered penalties, and with Zola he gave up all attacking free-kicks and corners. Yet still his influence wasn't reduced.

Of course, he had an early run-in with Gullit. The new manager had flexed his muscles by dropping Vialli at Leicester, then substituting Wise at half-time and leaving him out of the next game. Wise's anger was savage.

"Yes, I had a fall-out with Ruud," he says, still feeling the sharpness of the emotion. "And I learned a lesson! I wasn't playing well, maybe didn't deserve to play. But I just thought, if you get left out it means he wants to get rid of you.

"Ruud was a close friend of a bloke called Jim Creed, he used to play golf with him all the time and we'd talked and he spoke to Ruud, and Ruud said if he's worried tell him to come and see me. So I did and we had a long chat, Ruud said he wanted me to stay and wanted me to have a new contract. So we sorted everything out."

At the end of that season, he finally achieved his major Chelsea ambition. He lifted a trophy. The FA Cup was the first major trophy Chelsea had won for 26 years. They beat

Middlesbrough 2-0 in the final.

"We knew going into that that we were going to win it," he beams. "It's funny, but when that happens a lot of things go for you, and a lot of things went for us. Robbie scored so early, that settled us down, and we deserved to win."

The following season, 1997-98, Gullit withdrew him to the holding midfield role. The team was playing with a diamond and he had been on the left, but now in one of the most brilliant midfields the club has ever had – Wise holding, Dan Petrescu on the right, Gustavo Poyet on the left and Roberto Di Matteo at the front – he took on a new level of responsibility.

"Ruud wanted me to sit and dictate play, get the ball back and get it in to Robbie, Gus and Dan as soon as possible, and obviously to the little midget ahead – Franco. I enjoyed it.

"It was a very, very strong midfield. We rotated a lot, and you played with intelligence. They all had a lot of ability. The forwards got involved; defenders like Marcel and Frank Leboeuf could pass the ball and were happy to receive it at any stage. If you slightly mislayed a pass they'd touch it and make it look good.

"Gus played on the left side, Robbie played at the tip of the diamond and Dan on the right, and sometimes Gus played at the tip of the diamond and Robbie played on the left. It kept rotating. Or Dan in the middle and Robbie on the right.

"The only one who stayed in position was me, I'd sit and play them in. The system was suited for the players. The lads enjoyed passing it, playing football."

Gullit was controversially sacked, Vialli took over and it all became a little more professionalised if a little less explosive, and Wise continued to win, win, win.

In March 1998 there was the League Cup when he was Man of the Match in the final. Again, the opponents were Middlesbrough, and again it was 2-0. "I remember Gazza (Paul

Gascoigne) coming on and he smashed Eddie Newton, he really did smash him one and he'd only been on a minute. And I didn't want him thinking he was going to try and change everything, I did an awful tackle on him and he just couldn't believe it! But it was only because he'd smashed Eddie in the face with his arm!"

In extra-time Wise ran free to cross for Frank Sinclair to head the opening goal. After the game, he sent new manager Vialli up to be presented with the trophy. He was always thinking of others, thinking of the team. And he had his eyes set on a bigger catch.

Under two months later he was lifting the European Cup Winners' Cup. He overcame injury suffered in the dramatic semi-final win over Vicenza to lead his team to European glory. Again, he supplied the winner as Chelsea beat Stuttgart 1-0 in Stockholm. But, typically, he remembers it more for the scorer than himself.

"The midget's goal! What can you say? He came on for a minute, I've never seen him have so much passion in his body. It was quite scary. He was quite ugly!

"He was on 19 minutes and he won Man of the Match. And with a goal like that, he deserved it! It was unbelievable!"

Like Wise, Zola had overcome injury to be available for the final, but unlike him Vialli had left him on the bench. Now he was to make the difference.

"He came on, he lost the ball in midfield and it came to me, and it was open. He made a run and I played it in, and he could have controlled it but he half-volleyed it. It was only his second touch of the game and he pinged it in the top corner!" Wise underplays his part in the goal. His first-touch pass, perfectly weighted, perfectly placed, was a match-winning pass.

"It was a time when we were winning everything and doing really well. We really enjoyed the time."

In the double Cup-winning year, Wise was voted the club's Player of the Year for the first time. The next season started with a UEFA Super Cup win over Real Madrid. Three trophies in under six months!

"That was fun because Real Madrid expected to win." Vialli put him back to his old right-wing spot just to counter Roberto Carlos. Albert Ferrer, who didn't speak much English, was Chelsea's new right-back. Wise told him to hold his position, and he would always go with the runner. Ahead of Carlos was left-winger Savio. Wise was shocked at the amount of running he had to do. He had never encountered an athlete like Carlos before.

With over fifteen minutes left Madrid took off striker Mijatovic and put on a third left-sided player, debutant Robert Jarni. Wise looked across at Vialli on the bench and shouted: "Oi, I've had two ****ing whippets all night and now I've got three! What the **** do I do?"

Vialli just shrugged and laughed. They really were good times.

"They're president said afterwards to Ken Bates: 'Who's your Number 11?' And he said: 'It's our captain, Wise.' And he said: 'He kept upsetting our players, he kept kicking them!'" Happy days!

That year Chelsea made the best assault on the title since winning it in 1955. The team suffered just three League defeats and finished third, four points behind the champions. The title was still a possibility with a fortnight of the campaign to go.

There were some great performances. Wise the winner, however, chooses not to remember them. He is more matter-of-fact than bitter in his memories, but you can still detect the hurt.

"When we needed to be strong, we weren't. At home to West Ham (lost 1-0), 2-0-up against Leicester (drew 2-2), we weren't good enough at the right time. Those two games! We lost one and drew one. That really killed us!"

He dismisses his red cards which were being handed out more rapidly. "That's me unfortunately. If you take that away from me, I don't think I'd be half the player. It doesn't bother me. I paid a lot of fines to a lot of charities. There were some silly ones, but you do get that in life. I have been silly!"

But now that Chelsea were in the Champions League, World Cup-winning holding midfielder Didier Deschamps was purchased and Wise, aged 33, was made the attacking midfielder. He scored ten goals that season. There were crucial Champions League goals at Milan and Feyenoord, and at home to Marseille.

He was back on a lot of set-plays, especially corners. As he ran to take them, he would roar at the fans, demanding greater support. They always exploded into song. The relationship was at its peak.

Manchester United manager Sir Alex Ferguson accused him of being able to start a fight in an empty room. Early in the 1997-98 season he had been scratched badly down his face in the tunnel at Old Trafford by Nicky Butt. Now, in late 1999, he found his revenge, pinching Butt's thigh as they fell after a clash, and being kicked by the midfielder. Wise just smiled as Butt was sent off. Chelsea won 5-0.

But the League season petered out as the Champions League adventure went all the way to Barcelona in the quarter-final. In the end, however, there was more silverware. Aston Villa were beaten in the FA Cup Final, and once more he climbed the Wembley steps. But this time he took his four-and-a-half month old son Henry with him.

"That's the most memorable time of my career. After the game I said to Robbie, 'let's go and get the kids and take them up.' Gus took his up, Frank Leboeuf took his, and I took Henry. It was lovely. We took a bit of stick off the FA, but I don't care. It was the last Cup Final at the old Wembley, it will be with him for the rest of his life. I've got a lovely picture at home of us lifting the FA Cup."

For the FA Charity Shield victory the following August, he was back in defensive midfield. But that team was coming to an end. Vialli was sacked, Claudio Ranieri introduced, and Wise and the new manager never saw eye to eye. He remains frustrated that the title was never won.

"With the group of players we had, we were getting close, and we should have done it." Despite his loathing of Ranieri, in his final game, his 445th for the club, he scored his 76th goal and put the team on course to qualify for the UEFA Cup.

Dennis Wise is the fourth highest appearance maker in Chelsea's history. The six trophies he won as captain have only been equalled by John Terry since. The six he won as a player were only equalled at the time by Frank Leboeuf, Roberto Di Matteo and Gianfranco Zola.

Before he left he had a testimonial game and insisted the admission price be kept low so that children could come. After he left, he had an emotional return with Leicester at which he was given a legend's reception.

He is the club's 16th top scorer. Until Frank Lampard surpassed him, he was the top-scoring midfielder. Not bad for someone whose duties became increasingly defensive.

Henry, his son, trains in Chelsea's Academy. Dennis has moved on, but much of his heart, which with his feet and his tireless legs was his greatest commodity, has stayed at Stamford Bridge.

"I've got loads of friends from my Chelsea days, and also from my Wimbledon days. I'll always be friends with them, always get on with them. There's so many of that group.

"Enjoying myself, winning things, having good relationships with good people, that was what it was all about. I hope I helped a lot of people. I hope I made a lot of people enjoy themselves."

But despite having found all that for so long, the desire to win, the desire to do things his way, the desire to enjoy himself, made him leave aged 34 when the Ranieri revolution started. If in doubt, put your foot in!

"I had two years left on my contract as a player, and two more years as a coach! Crazy?"

You said it, Wisey!

Dennis Wise introducing Gianfranco Zola at a Chelsea dinner, 1998

"Now it's over to the midget for a few words. (Gianfranco gathered his thoughts. Dennis prompted) I just want to say... (Gianfranco repeated in a strong Italian accent: 'I just want to say...')...that I am the best player in the club...('that I am the best player in the club...')...and that all the others are 'sheet'! (and that all the others are sheet!')"

Dennis Wise writing to the fans in his captain's column in the matchday Champions League programme against Barcelona, 2000

"In my first FA Cup game for Chelsea we lost 3-1 at home to Oxford United. Now it's Barcelona at home, Newcastle at Wembley (in the FA Cup semi-final) and later Barcelona away. We've come a long way, you and us, haven't we?"

Gentleman, genius, giant smile

Gianfranco Zola

Welcome to Chelsea's most magical player from the club's most magical period.

For his team-mates it started on the first morning. Some training sessions become legendary within a football club. Gianfranco Zola's first at Chelsea was one such. The players knew someone special had entered their lives.

He had signed for almost a club record fee, £4.5m, despite being four months beyond his 30th birthday. It was before the days of the transfer window. His first session was on Tuesday 12th November, 1996. It was cold.

Over a decade on, Franco still smiles his giant smile, and his warm eyes twinkle as only his can when the subject is raised.

"I think maybe people were referring to the free-kicks," he says, polite of course, a little embarrassed to be talking about himself as ever, but in love with the life his Chelsea relationship still possesses. His huge white teeth are revealed in the almost-constant smile.

"Ruud made us take a few free-kicks. We were playing a game, there was a free-kick and he put a wall with three or four defenders in it and he told me to take it. I took my first and put it in the top corner. I took my second and put that in the top corner as well. I took five or six and all were on target. I was quite surprised as well. It was a very good training session."

For the fans it was six weeks later, on 21st December, 1996. This was Franco's first Chelsea game as a forward, partnering Mark Hughes. Until then he had played in midfield. After five minutes he had flicked on a Dan Petrescu cross and Hughes had opened the scoring against West Ham United. Four minutes later the moment came.

Player-manager Ruud Gullit was at sweeper and found Hughes with a good pass out of defence. Hughes hit a wonderful 30-yard pass to the diminutive, sprinting Zola who immediately ran at West Ham left-back and infamous assassin Julian Dicks from the front of the centre-circle. He turned inside and then, still on the sprint at the edge of the penalty area, stopped abruptly and ducked outside while flicking the ball away from Dicks and cutting quickly beyond. Then he let rip with a low cross shot that was in the net before anyone could take in quite what was happening.

Immediately, most Chelsea fans could pick out only a tiny selection of players who would have been capable of that, and none for a very long time. Here was skill, vision, pace and – that most important ingredient that only geniuses possess – the ability to do something that no-one watching or involved can anticipate.

Chelsea won 3-1. Gullit said afterwards: "Zola's was a very good performance. You can see that the crowd likes him. He stole their hearts in the way he plays. I think it was world class."

Team-mate and midfielder Craig Burley added: "The lads are all talking about Gianfranco in the dressing room, he was nutmegging people, scoring goals, setting goals up, back-heeling balls, he was just mesmerising people."

Chelsea fans were to be mesmerised for nearly seven more years as he became their most popular ever player. A vote on the club's official website in 2003 resulted in him being named Chelsea's best ever player. Two years previously, the whole

ground was singing: "One Mrs Zola, there's only one Mrs
Zola..." after the family had come to the decision to stay in
England, and at Chelsea, for another two years. It was an
extraordinary relationship between a very fulfilled crowd and a
very special person.

He made 312 appearances, scored 80 goals and brought a
new level of expectations and achievements to assists and
general forward team play. Not bad for a guy who was over 30
when he joined.

The 1996-97 campaign was a special period for both Chelsea
and all English football, and a special time in Great Britain as
well. There had been the successful hosting of the European
Championships in the summer of 1996. The population was
looking for change and in May 1997 voted for a different
government for the first time in 18 years.

Gullit had become manager in summer 1996 and introduced
"sexy football." The growl of the Eric Cantona-inspired
Manchester United was to be challenged by the smile of Zola
and, in the north-east at Middlesbrough, the smile of the
Brazilian Juninho who had arrived in October 1995.

The November explosion of Zola on to the scene brought
everything to a higher, new level. It was an extraordinary
transition for Chelsea.

Before Glenn Hoddle had become manager in 1993, support
was dwindling. Hoddle improved the quality of football, then
brought in Gullit and everyone started to love Chelsea.
Support not only grew but the club became a lot of people's
second favourite team. Then Gullit brought in Zola and it
wasn't just love at first sight with the players and fans, it was
love at first sight with the nation.

By the time he left Chelsea, it wasn't uncommon to see him
get a standing ovation from opposition supporters. With Zola,
values changed. And everyone smiled.

He came with a reputation of being a free-kick specialist.

"They were expecting me to produce that way and that was important," he admits.

In his first home game, against Newcastle United, he whipped in an arrow from wide on the left which Gianluca Vialli nudged into goal with a running header. In his second home game Everton were the visitors, and he scored his first goal with a rolling, dipping 35-yard free-kick. In his third home game he was pushed into attack and West Ham took the blows. He hit a unique run of form.

This was the year of the explosion of foreign imports. Chelsea already had a few: injured goalkeeper Kharine, defender Johnsen, midfielder Petrescu and Gullit himself, but that was it. Now Gullit had signed Leboeuf, Di Matteo and Vialli before Zola. All were smiling, talking, and easily adapting. The world was changing and people wanted to be part of what was happening in England, and especially at Chelsea.

Zola was carried away on a tide of love. "What happened to me was quite different and amazing. I came with a lot of willing to do well, I knew I was going through a difficult moment in Parma, and I came here with a determination to prove it was just a bad spell of my career.

"I was really lucky to find a fantastic atmosphere at the club. My team-mates were unbelievable. The crowd from the first day was fantastic. It made my life very easy. So all what became on the pitch was all a consequence of what I found outside."

What he found outside was nothing like he had ever experienced in Italy. Gullit had told him to come and enjoy the special English approach to the game. Before his first Christmas, he had no choice.

"I didn't expect to party with my team-mates when we went to a disco and Grodås nearly killed me, because I wasn't drinking at least a bottle of vodka."

The Norwegian goalkeeper Frode Grodås had also now joined and he and Erland Johnsen, directed by Dennis Wise, chased Franco to hold him down and force-feed him alcohol. Did they catch him and achieve their ends? The Norwegians say yes. Franco says no. Footballers!

Zola found an immediate ease in playing for Gullit. "He assured me it was going to be a good experience. On the pitch he had a great confidence in me. I really enjoyed playing for him. He was the kind of manager who asked the player to express himself. That is the kind of thing players like to hear."

Gullit was using the 3-5-2 shape he had inherited from Hoddle, and felt the tiny Zola – five feet six inches (1.68m), 10 stone 10 pounds (68kg) – would find forward play too physical. So he put him on the right of the central midfield three.

"Ruud said it was probably best for me," Franco says now. "Playing up front, he thought I couldn't get any space and would be under strict and close markers, he thought they would kick me. But Luca got injured, he had to play me in front and we found this perfect partnership with Mark Hughes.

"Mark was really important to me, he made my game easy, he was all the time creating space for me and for others. When you play with him it becomes easy. He used to run for his team-mates, and when there wasn't a hole he would create it! Smash the defenders!"

Franco laughs with much relish. Mark Hughes was his minder. As it turned out, however, Franco didn't need one. The rest of that season was mind-boggling.

December 26
Scored two goals at Aston Villa, Aston Villa 0 Chelsea 2.
January 26
Scored a fantastic left-footed volley equaliser as Chelsea came from two down in the fourth round of the FA Cup to beat Liverpool 4-2. He was also involved in creating the last two

goals. "The goal was very good, the game was fantastic, and for me that was the game when we won the FA Cup. Our performance in the second half was particularly special."

February 1

His cleverly disguised, chipped free-kick caused mayhem in the Tottenham defence and Chelsea took the lead with an own goal after 50 seconds at White Hart Lane, going on to win 2-1.

February 12

England 0 Italy 1, World Cup qualifier at Wembley.
Scorer: Zola.

February 22

At home to Manchester United with less than two minutes gone Zola received the ball wide, ran, stopped abruptly, cut inside Irwin who was left on his backside, stopped again and went outside Pallister whose knees seemed to knot, then when running square into the six-yard box just tucked the ball inside a frozen Schmeichel. United manager Sir Alex Ferguson was impressed: "Fabulous goal by Zola. He's a better player than I thought he was. We've watched him in the last three games and saw him against England. I felt he would play in a different type of way than he did today. In the Liverpool game he really played short of the strikers when he (Gullit) put Hughes and Vialli up. I felt if we played Roy Keane in that area, pushed my full-backs on and left Pallister and Johnsen to look after Hughes and Zola, we could cope with it. But he was clever enough to go wide and play out the sides and caused us lots of problems. So he's a clever little bugger." The strike won BBC's *Goal of the Month*. The game finished 1-1.

March 16

A wonderful scissor-kick volley from Dan Petrescu's cross opened the scoring in a 6-2 win at home to Sunderland.

March 19

A 25-yard missile was the only goal of the game at home to Southampton.

April 13

The semi-final of the FA Cup brought arguably the finest Zola goal – although he doesn't believe so. "Robbie (Di Matteo) got the ball 40 yards from goal and I made a run parallel to the edge of the box, and the ball was sent to me on the run. I controlled the ball with the heel, turned around, did it very well and got one metre on the defender, and I took a first touch and then beat him (the goalkeeper) with a shot." Genius! No-one could foresee as he ran that his first action would be a back-heel with no change of stride plus a turn and acceleration all before Wimbledon defender Blackwell could even slow down. Hughes joked: "He's given the lad twisted blood." It is a goal that still, when watched on a recording, defies easy explanation. It won the BBC's *Goal of the Month*. Chelsea won 3-0.

May 13

Having been in the country just six months, he became Chelsea's first-ever Footballer of the Year, and was presented with the award by Sir Stanley Matthews. He was truly humble. "It was something I wasn't expecting at all," he says now. "So many famous, talented players had it before me. I was so happy to receive it from Mr Matthews. It was something special. It was one of those moments you will remember forever."

May 15

Chelsea won major silverware for the first time in 26 years, the FA Cup. Zola set up the second goal in the 2-0 victory over Middlesbrough with an athletic back-heel. "We knew we weren't going to lose, not even if we played that match 100 times. It was our moment. Nobody could touch that moment. The second goal was a cross from Dan Petrescu which was a little bit too strong, but I believed in that, and I went with a back-heel. I just put the ball back and Eddie Newton was following the ball and scored. They ask me so many times, what was the best moment? Winning the FA Cup the first time, and the day after going on the Fulham Road was amazing. Honestly, I wasn't prepared for anything like that."

Amazing because of the mass crowds following the team, celebrating the team, and already in love with and in awe of the tiny player from Sardinia. Amazingly, this was only the beginning.

You don't get to be the most popular and the best player by being the nicest. Life's not like that. Gianfranco Zola is lovely, yes, but he's stubborn. He's proud, he's single-minded, he has had channel vision when he's felt challenged.

Few players had time for supporters like he did, the smile, the respect, the signature; few could melt hearts like he could, dedicating his goal to the memory of the recently lost David Rocastle, or to the young boy he had visited in a hospice a fortnight before; few could play with the sense of fairness and justice like him, with the smile and respect for opponents; and few could give time to the media like he always did after the most gruelling of games.

But when things weren't going right, he worked with a passion to make them turn. Nothing would be allowed to get in his way. It happened when he moved from Parma to Chelsea. It happened at the start and again at the end of his second season. It happened at the end of his fourth (2000) season and the end of his sixth (2002). Each time he turned things around.

He worked hard at training. He worked hard in preparation when he wasn't training. He focused his passion on himself in order to be better and better.

Meanwhile, he had come from a culture which went down in the penalty area if you were touched hard, and he won penalties that opponents moaned about. But he learned to play the English way and became even more admired.

Then there was the language issue. He didn't find English easy. "It was easy on the pitch, you don't need to talk very much," he insists. "It's just your bodies that talk. It was much, much easier on the pitch than outside!

"I found it much more easy to communicate with Wisey and Steve Clarke and Frank Leboeuf on the pitch than stepping out and having a conversation with them. It was very difficult with Dennis Wise and impossible with Steve, it was a long time before I could say something serious with them."

But he quickly became good friends with loud and crazy players, Wise, Gustavo Poyet; he became good friends with superstars, Gullit, Marcel Desailly; and most of all he became good friends with quiet ones, Kevin Hitchcock, Steve Clarke, golfers, two everyday guys who happened to be top footballers. Two guys like himself.

"I like easy, simple things, simple relationships," he says. "I don't like complicated things. I like good friendships. You don't choose a relationship by saying I'm going to be friends with him. It just goes naturally. I was very close to others too, Terry Byrne (head masseur), Gary Staker (player liaison officer), people like that."

He has remained close to all those people. They often visit him in summer.

Zola's second season didn't start as well as the first had finished. Gullit's pre-season training, which he had missed in 1996 by joining in November, was very ball-orientated and not as physically demanding as he was used to in Italy. He couldn't find full fitness and rhythm.

But the team was playing some extraordinary football and it was easy for him to join in with that. Slowly, his form turned. Suddenly he was at the hub of some of the most entertaining performances the club had ever produced. Chelsea won 6-0 at Barnsley, 6-1 at Tottenham, 4-1 at Sheffield Wednesday, 3-0 at

Crystal Palace; they won 7-1 at home to Tromsø, 4-0 to Derby, 4-2 to Southampton.

"It was probably the best football Chelsea had ever played," Franco believes. "Everyone was confident with each other. The passing, the mechanics were perfect. Everybody could have played with their eyes closed.

"It was just a pity we could not have had more consistency. You can't always have pretty and attractive football. We weren't able to win when we weren't playing good football."

Gullit was rotating the front two regularly for the first time, so Zola found himself playing with Vialli and new signing Tore Andre Flo as much as Hughes.

In November he scored his first and only first-class hat-trick in the 4-0 win over Derby. Two of his goals were outstanding, the last typically involving a wonderful back-heel in the build-up. He said afterwards: "The game, I think, must be sent to the schools. I don't want to exaggerate but it really was quality football."

In the victory at Tottenham he didn't score but, again typically, made four of the six goals. Yet that team stumbled in the New Year, Gullit was replaced and Vialli became player-manager. There was a positive reaction in the Cups, and in March Zola and Chelsea won a second trophy, the League Cup. In the final he hit the bar with a wonderful 25-yarder, and was involved in the build-up to both extra-time goals as Chelsea beat Middlesbrough 2-0 once more. It wasn't his greatest game but his work-rate was high.

Two weeks later he scored a powerful header in the dynamic European Cup Winners' Cup semi-final win at home to Vicenza – making the score 2-2 on aggregate but Vicenza having the away goal – and then celebrated Hughes hitting the ultimate winner. But nine days after that he tore his groin muscle, and with just two-and-a-half weeks to go to the final he looked a certain absentee.

Of course, he famously scored the winner. But the time between his injury and 17 seconds on the field before his goal, was as traumatic a time as he has had.

"I tore my muscle, and normally it takes four to six weeks to recover, so I was really in pieces when I was told that. I went to Italy to see my masseur and I started slowly, slowly working on it, and I was able in the end to be fit. And I was surprised then not to play because Luca said the day before I was going to play, and then made the team and I wasn't there."

Instead, along with Hughes, he was on the bench as Vialli himself and Flo started.

"I was really disappointed. So I stayed there and I was waiting, and waiting, and waiting, and the moment wasn't coming. Then when I came on I was so empowered I nearly broke the net. But I apologise for my celebration!"

He came on after 71 minutes. With his first touch he lost the ball but as it rebounded to Wise he made a dart for space near the penalty area. Wise played it in first-time, brilliantly, and as it bounced and it looked like sprinting Zola would take a touch, he unleashed a half-volley that was the equal of any goal he scored and more important than almost any other.

The celebration did require a bit of an apology, pumping legs and a fiercely thrusting finger at the supporters. No, I'm joking – and so was he! It's become a legendary celebration. But there was emotion in that moment beyond elation. Zola had been overlooked, Zola had arrived and made the difference!

He had been at Chelsea 18 months and had won three trophies after the team had won none for so long. In August he won a fourth, the Uefa Super Cup, setting up Gustavo Poyet to score the only goal of the match against Real Madrid in Monaco.

And in his third season Chelsea made a serious challenge for the championship for only the third time since winning it in

1955. The team lost just three League games all season. At that stage Chelsea were the sixth side in history to achieve such a record in the top flight. It was a real rarity. Zola was voted the club's Player of the Year, and was top scorer with 15 goals in all competitions.

Vialli had brought in fitness coach Antonio Pintus, and Zola felt the benefit. "For me it was going back to the Italian stuff. Before Pintus, physical-wise it wasn't very demanding. With Pintus it was good and it didn't take much to adapt. The other players appreciated his job, and it got better and better. It gave us a very different pre-season but it paid out."

There were some wonderful moments: his two goals in the 4-2 win at Leicester City, his chip over a spreading Schmeichel equaliser in the 1-1 draw with ultimate champions Manchester United at Old Trafford, his free-kick goals at Blackburn Rovers and at home to Aston Villa.

He formed an excellent partnership with Flo despite manager Vialli being concerned that the two were too alike, always wanting the ball to feet. Vialli was forced to play them together because of an awful injury to new signing Pierluigi Casiraghi, the Hughes replacement. Casiraghi was, and remains, one of Zola's closest friends.

"We missed very much Casiraghi," remains his first response to that special season. "He was an important player for us. In certain games having someone like him would have been very important. Despite me and Tore playing well that year, in certain situations he would have been vital.

"I played consistent football and was really tuned in. That year we were consistent as a team, and even when we were not playing well we were able to win."

Chelsea got into the Champions League for the first time, and at the age of 33 Zola embarked on a massive campaign. The team was well established and going for major trophies, bigger than anything won for almost 50 years.

It started magnificently. In the opening game Sunderland were beaten 4-0, and the fourth goal is widely regarded as one of Chelsea's best ever. Zola controlled a long pass from new signing Didier Deschamps, turned a circle to avoid a defender, saw Poyet making a run into the area and scooped a lob over the defence to fall into his stride and for him to scissor-kick dramatically into the roof of the net. He and Poyet always seemed to have a telepathic understanding.

"That was a great goal. There are things you cannot plan but are just so good to watch."

The Champions League was an extraordinary adventure. The opening 0-0 draw at home to Milan in which Zola starred and hit the post was thought by many to be some of the highest quality football ever seen at Stamford Bridge. The 5-0 win away to Galatasaray at their infamous "Stadium of Hell" was a result that shook the world of football. Chelsea had arrived in the big, big time. Zola opened up the defence for the first two goals by Flo and scored the third himself. When he went off with 15 minutes remaining, the crowd with the reputation for being the most hostile in Europe gave him a standing ovation. No-one in Istanbul could remember that happening before. He was very moved.

"That was a performance, by the way. We came out of that stadium which was very dangerous and very hot with all the applause of the stadium, so that tells clearly what we did that night. It was a fantastic performance."

There were more, especially the volley at Feyenoord to open the scoring when Chelsea qualified from the second group stage, and then the highly emotional and brilliant, brilliant 3-1 quarter-final home win over Barcelona: Zola opened the scoring with a trademark free-kick and raced away to set up the second for Flo.

But there was defeat in the second leg and as the season neared the end, all was not well. Chelsea lost 3-1 in normal time in Barcelona, 5-1 after extra time.

"That was hard to digest," he laments. "We started to play too late. We came back to 2-1 and Dani's header (seven minutes from time) destroyed us."

Domestically, Chelsea were not flourishing. Champions League qualification was missed. The Casiraghi replacement, record purchase Chris Sutton, had a poor campaign. Zola played mostly with Flo again. Flo scored a lot, especially in Europe, but in February Vialli signed former World Footballer of the Year George Weah, and for his arrival left Zola out of the squad altogether.

Zola, proud, stormed out of the stadium, thought better of his actions and collected a coat and returned to watch and support. It wasn't the first time he had felt hard done by. There had been the European Cup Winners' Cup Final. And he was being substituted often. One time the previous season, he had changed quickly and left after being dragged off, so he was away by the time the team returned to the dressing room. At the first subsequent training session he went round each player, shook their hand and apologised. Proud – and humble!

The problem for Zola in his fourth season was that despite lighting up Europe and creating so many goals, he wasn't scoring enough. In the end, Chelsea went and won the FA Cup. In the end, he played up front in the final with an out-of-form Weah – hard fate on Flo – and although the game was poor, Zola had a superb second half and took the free-kick which caused more mayhem and from which Di Matteo scored the only goal of the game. Aston Villa were beaten. Zola had his fifth medal.

But he had been hinting strongly it may be time to move on. He was going to be 34 in the summer, and it seemed Vialli was not enthusiastic to keep him. Glory and doubt were the clothes of Chelsea's greatest player in the summer of 2000 as yet another end-of-season open bus parade took place for the fans.

Gianluca Vialli, like Zola, is stubborn, proud and lovely too. He had not settled well as a player under Ruud Gullit. Now Zola was having the same problem under him.

Gullit had not wanted his forwards to work too hard when Chelsea didn't have the ball so that they would have a full capacity of energy when they were in possession. Vialli wanted them to work their socks off, be the first barrier of defence. Zola had suffered barren spells in his scoring, if not in his influence and creativity. Vialli had been more than rotating, he had been leaving him out of the side.

In the summer of 2000 it seemed certain the two would find it impossible to carry on working together.

Franco admits: "I was very close to leaving, and if it wasn't for Colin Hutchinson being there, he was the one who pushed with Luca to make me stay. In the end it was great that I stayed."

Managing director Hutchinson got Vialli, holidaying in Sardinia, together with Zola for a 90-minute meeting of straight talking, and the result was that Zola was to play on.

Now retired, Hutchinson says diplomatically: "Everybody was in agreement." But Vialli was clearly uneasy with the situation.

So pre-season started again, and again Zola found himself in partnership with a new signing. This time it was Jimmy Floyd Hasselbaink. The season kicked off with the Charity Shield at Wembley, and Chelsea beat Manchester United 2-0. A sixth trophy!

In the first League game Chelsea beat West Ham 4-2 and both Hasselbaink and Zola scored. But there were other difficulties in the camp, particularly between Vialli and Frank Leboeuf. The second League game was an unimpressive 2-0 defeat at Bradford City for which Leboeuf was internally suspended, and Vialli's post-match press conference suggested that some players weren't suited to playing away, or playing two games in a week.

For the weekend game, at Aston Villa, Zola was left out. It was a draw. At home to Arsenal the following midweek he returned and scored, but after leading 2-0 Chelsea were hauled back to 2-2. Away at Newcastle at the weekend he was dropped again, but with the score 0-0 came on with 10 minutes left. He did more in those 10 minutes than most of the other players achieved in the previous 80.

The media was ganging up on Vialli. Chelsea and Hutchinson wasted no time. The manager, the most successful in Chelsea history, was sacked. His replacement was Claudio Ranieri. The Italian was little known in England, but he was very well known to Zola. Ranieri had been head coach of Napoli when Zola was given the opportunity as a youngster to replace the departing Maradona. Ranieri had given him his big break in football. Now, aged 34, he was to give him a new life. But it wasn't an easy one.

Things didn't settle with Ranieri. He tried to build a squad with four senior players, Wise, Zola, Desailly and Poyet, but Wise and Poyet couldn't adapt to him and left at the end of the year along with Leboeuf. The great team of Gullit and Vialli was breaking up.

Chelsea went almost a year without winning an away game – no wonder Vialli had sought to address the problem in his own way – and Eidur Gudjohnsen had arrived to challenge for Zola's place with youth and strength.

Zola played in a variety of positions. Chelsea went out of the Cups early and struggled in the League. Towards the end of the campaign, with his contract coming to an end and his 35th birthday due, he and his family started thinking of home. Napoli took the hint and began pressurising to sign him.

It all became a very public dilemma. The Chelsea public went into overdrive and begged him not to go. The scenario, at times intense, went on for weeks. A dinner was held in his honour to try and persuade him to stay. But it wasn't an easy decision. His two young children were growing up more English than Italian.

In the end, once again, he found it impossible to leave. As the team fought for a Uefa Cup spot, he agreed to stay for a further two years, and if he finished playing then for two more years in an unspecified, non-playing role. This was his club, his adopted home.

Hutchinson had been determined to retain him. "I wouldn't take any offers from Napoli. And in the end they were all happy to stay."

In the final home game of the season, with Zola playing right-wing in a 4-2-4 formation, the Chelsea crowd displayed its gratitude to his wife by singing: "One Mrs Zola, there's only one Mrs Zola..." throughout the game.

Franco blushes at the memory even now. "It was one of the most embarrassing situations for my wife," he reveals. "And for myself! That was really, really embarrassing. I remember I was playing and I heard this song – normally I don't hear songs when I'm playing – but that caught my ear and I just started laughing.

"My wife said to me at the end of the game that she was in the Players' Lounge and she wanted to dig a hole."

The next game was at Liverpool, who were in a run of winning nine of their final ten games to win each of the League, FA and Uefa Cups and to qualify for the Champions League. The one game they didn't win was this home 2-2 draw with Chelsea. Michael Owen twice gave them the lead, Hasselbaink twice equalised, but the newly-settled Zola pulled the strings with a magnificent performance, and when he was substituted a minute from time the Anfield crowd gave him one of the most extraordinary ovations you could witness. At the sharp end of the season, that was yet one more special, special moment.

In the final game at Manchester City Chelsea qualified for the Uefa Cup, and everyone was just pleased to get away on holiday. With the old boys leaving and several new ones arriving, Frank Lampard, Emmanuel Petit, Boudewijn Zenden and William Gallas, plus John Terry and Carlo Cudicini forcing themselves into the side, it was a new team the next year.

It was often said Zola was Chelsea's finest ambassador, and that was how his final years were panning out. But there were further difficulties that next year. In 2001-02 he ceased to be first choice.

"It wasn't easy," he admits. "Eidur and Jimmy were playing very well together and they were scoring a lot of goals. I had started the season playing well but not scoring very much, and in the end it was right to play those two."

He scored only five goals, and although he appeared in 50 games he started only 28 of them. It was his worst year at the club. Yet it will be remembered for one moment, and most people – including him – would argue his greatest in terms of goalscoring.

At home to Norwich in the FA Cup, the team was leading 2-0 with just over an hour gone. "That was something special – like the goal against Sunderland that was special!" he says with pride. "You don't plan that, it's more instinct. Graeme Le Saux took this corner and as usual he mis-hit it..." he is joking and beams his giant smile, "...but I believed in that, and actually I went to head it, but it was low and instinctively I just tried to back-heel it. To be honest, I have to say I was very lucky for the ball to go into the top corner."

The 24,231 crowd didn't really appreciate the aerial ballet and unique technique until the goal was reshown on the big screen. He had leapt high and back-flicked a volley from a ball travelling at pace. By now, Zola couldn't suppress the big smile. It was a goal that was celebrated twice in seconds, and the second time on the action replay even more than the first. This was genius in its veteran years. Or we thought its veteran years.

After the game the media world wanted to talk to the man of the moment. He dedicated the goal to Matthew Aston, a boy he had visited in a hospice two weeks before and who since had died of a brain tumour. He dedicated it to him especially, and to his parents.

There are rarely moments like these in football.

Chelsea reached the FA Cup Final. Zola left the substitutes' bench to replace the injured Hasselbaink midway through the second half with the score 0-0, but this time there was to be no fairytale finish. Arsenal won 2-0.

Perhaps people thought that this would be the end of the 35-year-old. He would be 36 when the next season kicked off. How wrong such people were!

"I used the situation in a positive way," he says. "I promised myself that next year I'm going to come back and get my place back, and I told that to the second man (Angelo Antenucci) at the last game. 'Next year you're not going to see me on the bench a lot.'

"I worked all summer in Sardinia. I worked most on the mental side. I knew I was going to face a difficult situation, and most of all the strength had to come for that. I got very much into yoga. It improved my capacity of concentration. I found a friend to improve my techniques of concentration. And most of this was the determination that I didn't want to end my stay at Chelsea with that season. It was like going back to school again.

"And that final year is one of the years I am most proud of, because it wasn't easy. Most people were going to bet against me. I was already 35 and about to be 36. People said I was on my way down and I should pack up. But I said I can't pack up like this.

"I worked very hard, but when you work hard and it pays off – how well you feel it!"

Chelsea had pre-season difficulties. The club had gone broke. After a succession of heavy-spending summers, no money was spent at all. And although it wasn't publicised, Champions League qualification was required to prevent a massive sale and possible financial ruin.

Hasselbaink and Gudjohnsen had pre-season difficulties with fitness. Thirty-six year-old Zola hit the ground running.

"I think that was my best season. My legs weren't the same but my mental strength was much bigger than before. I was a mental player. That pre-season I scored the most goals ever, something like ten in five games. They were friendlies, but for me it was important because I was already building up my confidence."

The magician scored eight in the first ten League games. He was running games and making goals. When in early December he orchestrated the League Cup demolition of Everton 4-1, he revealed he was talking about yet another new contract and was of a mind to play on.

"When you get it going then it becomes easy to play your best football. I started very well and never lost a grip of it."

He scored some exceptional goals, including one in a marvellous 15-minute spell of skills and influence during the 2-0 win at West Bromwich Albion which again resulted in a standing ovation from home fans which started while he was on the ball in open play.

Once again there were to be no trophies under Ranieri, but as the team homed in on its second Champions League qualification the manager returned to the strength of Hasselbaink and Gudjohnsen, and for the last two home games Zola had to start on the bench. His new contract hadn't yet materialised. Once more it was looking as though this could be the end. He wanted to play on, so no thoughts of a non-playing role were in his head.

At home to Everton he came off the bench to score what turned out to be his final Chelsea goal. It was superb. "I think it was a long pass from the defence, and I just ran on to it, and the goalkeeper was coming out but realised he was late. He tried to go back but I didn't give him time and one-touch just flicked it over him." That touch was from an acute angle with the outside of his right boot. He smiled and smiled at the fans in the Matthew Harding Stand.

And so to the final shoot-out! Chelsea had to draw at home to Liverpool to qualify for the Champions League. If Liverpool could win, they would finish fourth above Chelsea and qualify.

"I played the whole season and Ranieri said to me, 'today is a particular game, you're not playing.' Well, I said 'okay, I'm not very happy, but if it is good for the team then no problem. I will wait and if you need me you know where I am.'

"But when I went on the bench I was shaking, not because I was cold, but tension. I had a lot of nerves. So when I came on my legs were jelly for the first minute."

He came on for the last 20 minutes with Chelsea winning 2-1. Towards the end he received the ball on the left touchline, and pirouetting and dancing simply kept it from frustrated Liverpool players as four, five challenges came diving in. Oh how the crowd roared and sang his name and laughed as precious time was used up. It was just about his last meaningful action for Chelsea, and it was one of the most entertaining pieces of action of the season.

"Well, I got the ball in there and I knew I had to keep it, so I concentrated on keeping it but they were coming for my legs so I had to avoid them, and I kept the ball for a while and it was quite remarkable action."

He won Player of the Year for the second time. He was top

scorer. But the new contract offer never arrived. It wasn't the most dignified of endings. Senior players like him and Le Saux were allowed to drift away. His home island club Cagliari moved in for his services. He was about to turn 37. When nothing happened, he agreed to move.

And as he did, Roman Abramovich bought Chelsea. It was too late to rescue Zola. Abramovich looked into buying Cagliari. But the era of the greatest magician was over. These days, when he comes to Stamford Bridge, it's normally to sit in Abramovich's box and enjoy the game with him.

He came at the top, he went out at the top, and he watches at the top.

Needless to say, Zola did not allow an empty goodbye. He organised a press conference for a Monday in the following pre-season at Stamford Bridge. But he arrived on the Friday and went and lunched with the players on the Saturday. He met his golf pals on the Sunday.

He spent over an hour with the press. Unbelievably, at the end they burst into applause and stood for him. It was standing ovations to the end. Then they moved forward to shake his hand. No-one had witnessed anything like it before. He moved out and gave all assembled Chelsea fans as much time as was needed. And he finally gave his final goodbyes.

Well, not quite. He was in the crowd at Lazio supporting Chelsea in the Champions League the following October, and after going to see the players in the dressing room afterwards he was dragged by John Terry back on to the pitch and paraded before the travelling Chelsea fans.

Then, the next August, he attracted a full Stamford Bridge house to a farewell game. He spoke to the crowd afterwards, standing on the pitch with a microphone, and thanked them for everything.

I hope you lived through Zola. If you did, I know you are smiling now.

**Gianfranco Zola saying goodbye to the fans on Chelsea
TV following his seven years at Chelsea**

"It's been truly a pleasure and an honour to play for this club
and this shirt. I've played good games and I've played bad
games, but I always played with passion and care, and what
I've received here goes beyond what I was expecting."

Gianfranco Zola, again saying goodbye

"The people they stop me and they say 'thank you for
everything you've done for this club,' but it should be me
saying thank you to them for what you made me become. And
I do believe that!"

**Tore Andre Flo when at Sunderland and asked by his
club to look at a video of his goals for Chelsea to learn
why he wasn't scoring for them**

"I told them that every time I made a run there was a little
man on the ball with his head up looking for me and ready to
make the perfect pass.

The Zola Years

1997	Footballer of the Year, FA Cup winner, FA Charity Shield runner-up;
1998	League Cup winner, European Cup Winners' Cup winner, Uefa Super Cup winner;
1999	Chelsea Player of the Year, qualified for Champions League;
2000	FA Cup winner, FA Charity Shield winner;
2002	FA Cup runner-up;
2003	Chelsea Player of the Year, qualified for Champions League.

Jimmy Greaves in warm-up mode at Stamford Bridge, 1957

Jimmy Greaves earned a big-money move to AC Milan due to his goalscoring exploits at Chelsea, while (below) Peter Bonetti thwarts Manchester United's George Best

Peter Bonetti shows safe hands against Leeds United
in the 1970 FA Cup Final replay at Old Trafford

Celebrations in the bath after victory in the 1970 FA Cup Final - left to right:
Tommy Baldwin, John Hollins, Peter Bonetti, David Webb, Peter Osgood

Peter Osgood's diving header beats Leeds United goalkeeper David Harvey
to bring Chelsea level in the 1970 FA Cup Final replay at Old Trafford

Left to right: Eddie McCreadie, Peter Bonetti, Peter Osgood, Charlie
Cooke and Alan Hudson walk out at Stamford Bridge

71-72, left to right: Bonetti, Hinton, Mulligan, Houseman, Cooke, Garland, Dempsey, Osgood, McCreadie, Phillips, Baldwin, Harris, Boyle, Kember, Webb, Hollins, Hudson

A break from training, left to right: Mulligan, Harris, Osgood, Hollins, Garland, McCreadie, Webb, Dempsey, Bonetti, Hinton, Kember, Cooke, Hudson

Charlie Cooke in action (top), and (above) taking on Stoke City's
Alan Bloor during the 1972 League Cup Final at Wembley

Recording of club anthem *Blue Is The Colour* ahead of the 1972 League Cup Final, including Perfect 10 players Charlie Cooke (second left) and Peter Osgood (third right)

Chelsea players, including a topless Kerry Dixon (centre) hail the fans from the front row of the directors' box after clinching promotion with a 5-0 victory over Leeds United

Kerry finds the target in the 5-3 win against Fulham at Craven Cottage, October 1983

On target against Derby County in 1990 - Kerry celebrates, to the disgust of Mick Harford and (below) Dennis Wise and cardboard cutout revel in Cup success, 1997

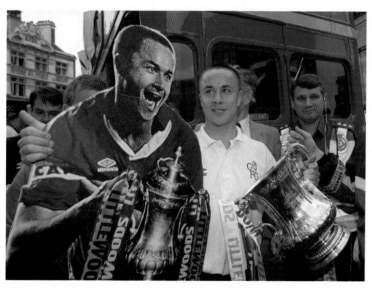

The skipper congratulates goalscorers Roberto Di Matteo (left) and Eddie Newton following the 1997 FA Cup Final victory over Middlesbrough

Dennis lifts the 1998 European Cup Winners' Cup following victory over VfB Stuttgart, and (below) celebrating the '98 Super Cup defeat of Real Madrid with Gianfranco Zola

Gianfranco Zola celebrates a goal with Dennis Wise, while (below) future star Joe Cole consoles the Italian after the Hammers secured a shock 3-2 victory at Stamford Bridge

John Terry celebrates the Champions League winner against Barcelona in
2005, and (below) with Frank Lampard, lifting the FA Cup in 2007

John Terry lifts the Premiership trophy in 2005 - Chelsea's first top-flight title in 50 years

Frank Lampard shows his delight after scoring the winner against Aston Villa, 2005

Frank levels matters in the Champions League Final against
Manchester United in Moscow's Luzhniki Stadium, May 2008

Joe Cole celebrates his winner over Liverpool at Anfield, New Year's Day 2005 while (below) he receives the acclaim of the crowd against Blackburn the following season

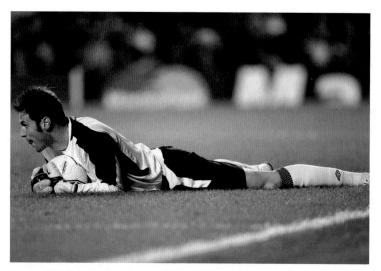

Petr Cech shows a safe pair of hands against FC Porto, September 2004
while (below) he denies Middlesbrough's Stewart Downing, February 2006

(Left to right) John Terry, Petr Cech and Ricardo Carvalho celebrate European
Champions League semi-final success over Liverpool at Stamford Bridge, April 2008

Born was the King of Stamford Bridge

Peter
Osgood

Five minutes to three o'clock, Saturday afternoon, Stamford Bridge. Second half of the 1960s, first half of the 1970s.

Ron Harris, captain, led Chelsea out to the pitch at a trot. Goalkeeper Peter Bonetti was second. Centre-forward Peter Osgood was third. Bonetti ran to the goal, the Shed crowd called his name and he waved. Osgood ran to the edge of the six-yard box and started warming Bonetti up with short, sharp shots at goal. The Shed sang his song.

It went to the tune of *The First Noel*. It was just the chorus, but later it got a verse. Mostly, though, just the chorus was used. But let's have the lot here:

> *And out from the Shed*
> *There rose a young star*
> *Scoring goals past Pat Jennings*
> *From near and from far.*
> *And Chelsea won*
> *Like we all knew they would*
> *And the star of that great team*
> *Was Peter Osgood.*
>
> *Osgood, Osgood, Osgood, Osgood,*
> *Born is the King of Stamford Bridge.*

Osgood, Osgood, Osgood, Osgood,
Born is the King of Stamford Bridge.

It was only as the final rendition of the chorus was coming to an end that 'the King' languidly raised his arm and saluted the Shed. His Shed!

Peter Osgood was born in 1947. He wasn't a Chelsea supporter when he went for a trial in 1964. But he went on to play 380 games, score 150 goals, and be the first centre-forward to lead Chelsea to winning the FA Cup and the first to lead them to a European trophy. He was outrageously talented and sometimes outrageous in his behaviour. He was a top entertainer. In his retirement he followed Chelsea out of love and for a living. He died suddenly, aged 59, in 2006. At Stamford Bridge, his ashes are buried below the penalty spot at the Shed End and his name is still sung at every game. He remains the King.

The swagger! No-one else had his swagger. Six feet two inches, strong, the lightest of touches on the ball when required: right-foot, left-foot, headers, control, he had everything but burning pace. And he knew it. In the modern and recent game, only Eric Cantona at Manchester United has had anywhere near that swagger.

And, as with Cantona, he could be naughty. He knew how to look after himself. Sometimes he went too far – both on the pitch and off it. That just made the fans worship him all the more.

Down the years he has given me many interviews (we have had many drinking sessions too, but who didn't have those with the King?). In one, he said: "I'm very privileged, I scored in every Cup final I played for Chelsea. I'm that sort of player, they look for the big occasion. I've got to admit I didn't turn it on week in, week out. But on the big occasion I was ready."

Osgood on the big occasion

1964 South-East Counties Floodlit Cup Final second leg:
West Ham Youth 1 Chelsea Youth 3 (scored 2).
1964 London Challenge Cup Final:
Brentford Reserves 2 Chelsea Reserves 1 (scored).
1970 FA Cup Final replay:
Chelsea 2 Leeds United 1 (scored Chelsea's equaliser).
1971 European Cup Winners' Cup Final:
Chelsea 1 Real Madrid 1 (opened scoring);
Replay, Chelsea 2 Real Madrid 1 (scored Chelsea's second).
1972 League Cup Final:
Chelsea 1 Stoke City 2 (scored Chelsea's equaliser).

In the days when players went out and just played and there was little communication between them and the fans, Ossie was at the front guard of change. He promised in the media that when he scored his 100th League goal against Everton he would do a lap of honour after the game. He scored twice that day.

Hardly a soul left the ground on the final whistle. He walked to the tunnel as if he'd forgotten, his anthem ringing in his ears from the Shed, and then when he reached the side of the pitch he set off, around the old Stamford Bridge dog track, blowing kisses to the fans. He was unique. But that's no surprise – that is what kings are.

When Ken Bates was chairman of Chelsea, after Osgood had retired, Bates loved (with good reason) his centre-forward Kerry Dixon. One day he asked me: "I'm not being funny, but Kerry's scored more goals than Osgood, why do the fans love him so?"

Kerry was a great goalscorer, no doubt. But Ossie was a great footballer. Ossie used to tell Kerry that he had got all his Chelsea goals in the top flight. The two became good friends towards the end of Ossie's life, and the King turned out free for Kerry, speaking at a fundraiser at his local club Dunstable. The mutual respect was probably as much for each other's love of Chelsea in retirement as for achievements on the pitch.

Osgood did everything in life with a passion. It was all or nothing. When it was 'all', there was no-one better. And there was enough of that in his wonderful career for him to retain his legendary status nearly 30 years after retirement.

Peter Osgood, aged fifteen, didn't get selected in a trial at Reading, then refused to go for a trial at Arsenal on the grounds that he'd embarrass himself after being by-passed at Reading. But he couldn't get out of a trial at Chelsea.

He was scoring around forty goals a season for his club near Windsor, Spital Old Boys. He had applied for his trial at Reading. The Spital club secretary had applied for the Arsenal one. His uncle applied for the crucial trial at Chelsea.

"They called me The Man From Uncle," Ossie laughed, recalling the famous 1960s television series. "Bob Snaishell married my mum's sister, he's Chelsea mad! His house is called 'Win Chelsea'. He wrote in for a trial and didn't even tell me. Because he was my uncle I couldn't duck out of it.

"I went for a trial at Hendon and there were about 150 boys. I thought I didn't have a chance. Really! But after half-time Dickie Foss (youth-team coach) pulled me and said: 'You gotta sign, son.' I said: 'Why are you doing this Mr Foss?', and he said, 'well, there's ten scouts here and they all want to sign you.' It was unbelievable."

He became an amateur and played his first game away to Portsmouth juniors and scored a hat-trick, then was drafted back into the team for the second leg of the Southern Junior Floodlit Cup Final at West Ham for whom Harry Redknapp was playing, and notched two.

In his fine autobiography, *Ossie, King of Stamford Bridge*, he recalled: "The next day on the building site Dad was bubbling over, but for the other brickies, chippies and labourers the Southern Junior Floodlit Cup meant nothing and I kept tight-lipped about it. At lunchtime, though, when we sat down to eat our sandwiches and crack open the thermos flasks, one of the labourers unfolded his *Daily Express* and there was a decent match report with my name in the headline: 'New boy Osgood shines'. I had to look at it two or three times for it to sink in. Perhaps it was at this point that I stopped being Peter Osgood and became *Peter Osgood*."

The following season he turned full-time and by Christmas, aged seventeen, had made his first-team debut. In another year, his name was being established throughout Europe. It was a meteoric change of life.

The man behind it was manager Tommy Docherty. "I still call him boss today," Ossie said not long before his death. The manager wanted to introduce him to first-team culture in the fifth round of the League Cup, away to Workington Town. "Tommy Doc took me along there, I was sitting in the dug-out, it was a terrible result. I think they were Fourth Division and we drew two-each. We got hammered.

"I came back and played in the replay and scored two goals in front of 7,000 people." Actually, it was 7,936. This was his debut. Both goals came in the last ten minutes. In his autobiography, Osgood remembers those first two of 150 magical moments. "George Graham glided through and found me with an intelligent pass on the edge of the area. I slipped through and swerved right past the advancing Workington keeper, and clipped the ball across him and into the back of the net. I had no time to savour the moment because before we knew it Tommy Knox had thumped another shot against the post and I was there to tap it firmly home. After the game the players and Tommy himself hugged me and ruffled my hair, like you do a kid."

At this stage Osgood was tall, lithe, fast, mobile – he was electric. But he wasn't strong. He was like a panther, stalking in search of action, preserving his energy for the moments of explosion. He was averaging more than a goal a game in the reserves, but he didn't play in the first team again that season. Chelsea went on to lift the League Cup, but youngsters like Jim McCalliog and his new close friend John Boyle saw more action than he did.

As with Jimmy Greaves over seven years before him, his life was both simple and becoming complicated. Simple: working-class background, having some fun, enjoying his football. Complicated: marrying young, starting a family by eighteen. Also like Greaves, there was a lot of travel involved. Greaves came from Essex, Osgood from outside Windsor. Curiously, Osgood and Greaves shared the same birthday, February 20th. Spooky!

Early in the 1965-66 season Osgood was given his League debut by Docherty, but he went straight back to the reserves. Kings do not get crowned too easily! Osgood revealed in his autobiography that the curse that was to target him all his career started young. 'Docherty told me he thought I didn't try hard enough. Where had I heard that before? It was a refrain that had been with me all my life, and it would stay with me for the rest of it. Even Dad, my biggest fan, tried to gee me up and get me to run around the park more. Everyone, it seemed, wanted me to break into a sweat but my style of play had got me this far and what didn't come natural didn't seem right to me. The manager said I was sluggish in training and ordered me back in the afternoons when the other lads had returned to their wives, bars or golf courses, for extra running, weight work and the dreaded 'doggies'.'

It must have worked. A couple of weeks later Docherty called him in again. "The boss said to me, 'Look, I've got some strong players here but I think you're going to make it.

I'm going to give you ten games. I don't care how you play. The crowd will give you some stick because Barry Bridges is a big favourite here.' That's awesome for a kid. Barry Bridges was England centre-forward at the time and he put him on the right-wing. I love Barry, he was great for me in the dressing room, all the lads were, Terry Venables, Bert Murray. Ten games: there's no pressure on you and it went from there."

Bridges had already won three caps. He wasn't happy. "I had a little bit of a personal thing when he first came into the side," the Norwich-born and now retired newsagent admits from his Norwich home, "because he took my place, and you knew I wasn't going to get back in place of him. As it was, Frankie Blunstone got injured and I got back in the side. But he was a great player, a fantastic player."

Ossie believed he was helped in it all being so easy. "I went into a good side. It's very hard to go into a side that's struggling. And let's be honest, Bonetti, Tambling, Bert Murray, Bridges, Venables, McCreadie, all these boys, they were homegrown or arrived young, they absolutely adored Chelsea. That was the thing in those days, they didn't want to play for anyone else. You had Harris, Boyle, so many."

No-one adored him more than Docherty: "Skill, a great attitude, two great feet, good in the air, a marvellous heart...what more is there?"

He had played the home leg of the massive Inter-Cities Fairs Cup opener against Roma when Chelsea won 4-1 and Venables scored a hat-trick. He had played the next game too, but then Bridges played the following four. Now he got his Docherty promise.

Chelsea lost 2-0 at home to Leicester City with Bridges a substitute. There were fan protests. Bridges asked for a transfer. But then Chelsea won 2-1 at Sheffield United and Osgood got his first League goal. Some good results but no more goals followed until a 4-2 win at Villa Park four games later. "I scored a blinding goal. There was a light snow and when the ball came to my feet not far past the halfway line I began to run forward with no real purpose in mind. I beat two Villa defenders, dummied another and, before I knew it, it was just me and the goalie and I smashed past him with such force that the ball hit the net and rocketed straight out again."

Already there was less talk about Bridges and people were sitting up and looking at Osgood. In the second leg of the Inter-Cities Fairs Cup second round, the next game, he netted with a wonderful, powerful diving header against Wiener Sport-Club. He used to get ribbed that this and the Cup Final Replay goal were his only diving headers. Ossie didn't always do diving!

In December, Bridges got his right-wing berth and started scoring from there. Osgood looked set to keep the No. 9 shirt.

Three consecutive games in the New Year sealed his ascendancy to the throne. At home to Tottenham Hotspur, Chelsea were behind to a Dave Mackay penalty. "Nearly 50,000 were crammed in and witnessed me lay on an equaliser for George Graham and then score the winner with a 25-yard shot that rocketed into the top corner of the net, leaving Big Pat rooted to his line."

Scoring goals past Pat Jennings
From near and from far.

Next up was an FA Cup third-round trip to holders Liverpool. Roger Hunt scored for them in the first minute. Osgood equalised six minutes later. Chelsea went on to win with a Bobby Tambling goal, their first win at Anfield since 1935. The third game was a 2-1 victory at Burnley and he got both goals, including one that numerous witnesses claim was the best of his career. Sadly, there were no television cameras available to capture it.

Burnley, at this stage, were still a top club, on their way to finishing third that season behind Liverpool and Leeds United. "I picked the ball up in my own half, beat Merrington, Talbot and John Angus, the Burnley defenders, and outpaced some others before driving it past Adam Blacklaw, the goalkeeper, as he came out to block me off."

Bonetti recalls: "It was a cracking goal, the best I saw him score. There were very, very muddy conditions, horrible conditions, nothing like the pristine pitches nowadays, and he picked it up around the halfway line and zig-zagged past five or six players and smashed it in the net. Ossie wasn't a stamina-type of player, but it took everything to score that. It was remarkable."

Osgood, Osgood, Osgood, Osgood
Born is the King of Stamford Bridge.

He made his England U23 debut against Scotland at Roker Park and scored. Then, after Leeds had been beaten for the second time in the season, in the FA Cup on this occasion, he scored another outstanding goal, and this one was televised. It was at home to Milan in the Inter-Cities Fairs Cup third round, second leg. "I scored some good goals," he told me, "and AC Milan was one of the best, an unbelievable half-volley. We won 2-1. George Graham scored. I played against Schnellinger, Maldini, fantastic names that roll off your tongue. It was a great experience for such a young lad.

"Playing up front with George Graham, George was fantastic! They called him 'Stroller' when he went to midfield, but he was great to play up front with. He was strong, he could hold the ball up, he could lay the ball off, he was a great foil for me."

Graham laughs now at the compliments. "He was 100 per cent right!" And then he returns them. "I was only about twenty-one when Ossie came. We all wondered who this gangly, tall boy was. But right away you knew he was special. Ossie was a young Rolls Royce, when he moved with the ball he was poetry in motion. Some of the games he played he was just magic.

"And because he was tall he was just so elegant. That was him. Elegance! This elegance, running with the ball, definitely magic! He came from non-League almost right into the Chelsea first team. He was one of the best 19-year-olds I've ever seen, and I've seen a few: Wayne Rooney, Ryan Giggs, Charlie George, David Rocastle.

"Ossie was a natural. He learned and improved with coaching, but to come through at that age without professional coaching was a fantastic achievement."

When England manager Alf Ramsay named a squad of forty in advance of the World Cup, Osgood was included. At nineteen years of age, he was approaching the top of the tree. He didn't make the final twenty-two, but he was already recognised as one of the top players in the country.

The domestic goals dried up a little, but he scored the winner against Munich 1860 which took Chelsea to their first European semi-final. However, the team, still brittle from the Blackpool affair a year before when eight players had been sent home by Docherty, fell apart. He lost his first FA Cup semi-final to unfancied Sheffield Wednesday, and lost to Barcelona in a play-off in the European game. That was the last match of the season and was preceded the night before by a night on the beer by several players. Chelsea finished sixth in the League. Docherty sold Venables, Bridges and Murray, bought Charlie Cooke, and early the following season was forced to swap Graham with Tommy Baldwin at Arsenal.

Osgood had loved the company of Venables and Graham, but Cooke and Baldwin became good, heavy drinking replacements. And they could both play too. By October 1st

1966, Chelsea were top of the League. They went there with a 4-1 win at Manchester City. Osgood, still nineteen, scored his sixth goal of the season. Debutant Baldwin, Tambling and full-back Kirkup were the other scorers.

The following Wednesday Chelsea went to Blackpool for a League Cup tie. When Osgood told this version of events, Emlyn Hughes had already died. "Emlyn came and sorted me out, bless him. I've never really had that big a grudge against him, but he did come to hurt me!" Hughes' challenge broke Osgood's leg badly. He was out for the season.

"Unfortunately, I went out and started playing golf on crutches with my Uncle Bob, and I was out for a year. I put on about two-and-a-half stone in weight, it set me back. Everyone said I wouldn't be the same player, but I had a good football brain. You had to be quick and you had to be clever."

Chelsea replaced him with Tony Hateley, a record signing. The football disintegrated. The team finished ninth. But it fought its way to its first Wembley FA Cup Final, only to lose to Tottenham. Hateley was sold in the summer. The world prepared for the return of the King.

He started the 1967-68 season but he found it hard to rediscover the magic. The change of body shape was remarkable. He always fought the assumption that it came from drinking.

"It runs in the family, it's not the way I lived. I drink a dry white wine now and it still doesn't work." He'd point to his belly and laugh. However, when he first changed to wine he used to joke that instead of drinking six pints a night he drank six bottles! Once retired he lived off his bad boy name on the after-dinner circuit, but he always wanted to be remembered as a serious professional. "I played hard and I lived hard. All the boys did. Everybody says that they train harder now – they don't train harder today than we did! We used to do a cross-country over Epsom Downs every Tuesday, four-and-a-half, five miles. The only thing is Dave (Sexton) had to wait for Marvin Hinton and me because we were about twenty minutes behind everyone else. But we did it. We did 440s, cross-country, everything."

He'd delight in the story of letting the players get ahead of him and he'd watch them tear off on a circular cross-country run while he hid in the bushes with Hinton, and then the two rejoined them from behind again on the way back, but in truth that was not what normally happened.

Yet there is no doubt that the drinking during the year of rehabilitation took its effect. However, he always denied that he was part of the real high-life living style of some of the others. "I was a country boy. Huddy (Alan Hudson), Charlie Cooke, Tommy Baldwin, they were the Herberts! They were the boys! I lived in Windsor. After an away game me and Marvin Hinton would have a few drinks and stay in the Ifield (the pub round the corner from Stamford Bridge), but that was it."

On his return, it wasn't only him struggling – it was the whole team. The disintegration, rather than the Cup form, had carried over. At the beginning of September, after a 5-1 defeat at Newcastle United, Chelsea lost 6-2 at home to Southampton. Ironically, there was a chink of light in the game for Osgood. He got both goals. "One of them was one of the best I ever scored at Stamford Bridge. I swayed past five Southampton players."

But he couldn't follow it up, and Chelsea couldn't improve. By the end of the month, Docherty was gone. Chelsea's first game with new manager Dave Sexton in charge resulted in a 7-0 defeat. The night before Osgood and Eddie McCreadie, saddened by the departure of a manager they revered, had gone on a heavy drinking session. The way forward was established.

"Dave was fantastic. He was a brilliant coach. You looked forward to training. The only thing was he couldn't handle players." Sexton rejuvenated Chelsea and they finished fifth and reached the quarter-finals of the FA Cup. Osgood scored seventeen goals. But the new manager wasn't happy with the team.

He started buying less fanciful, less visionary artists, and tried to work bullish grafters into the side. He wasn't happy with his midfield either. He had been coach to Docherty a couple of years earlier, and didn't feel Cooke had replaced Venables. So when Osgood had a dry run the following season, he moved Cooke to the wing, Osgood back into midfield and used newly-signed Alan Birchenall and Tambling in attack. 'Dave signed Alan Birchenall, a striker from Sheffield United,' Osgood wrote typically entertainingly in his autobiography, 'whose most distinctive feature was his blond hair; personally, I thought he was a ringer for Mae West, only more feminine!'

Osgood did well in the role, creating more than scoring, but still finishing the campaign with thirteen goals. The problem was that the team finished fifth and went out of the FA Cup in the quarter-final again. Another big, bullish striker had been bought, Ian Hutchinson, so now Hutchinson, Birchenall, Baldwin and Tambling were vying for the centre-forward places.

The FA Cup had become the Holy Grail for the club. As it started its 65th year, the League had been won once, and the FA Cup never. The League got off to an awful start, a 4-1 defeat at Liverpool. Osgood was poor in midfield. One game later he was dropped. For weeks Sexton toyed with the side, unable to find a combination that worked. He tried Baldwin, Hutchinson and Tambling up front, he tried Birchenall in there, he threw in Osgood. Osgood started scoring as soon he was put back in attack. Then, on November 8th 1969, it happened.

For the first time he paired Osgood with Hutchinson in attack, and behind them played a midfield of Cooke, John Hollins, 18-year-old Alan Hudson and Peter Houseman. Chelsea won 3-1 at Sheffield Wednesday with Osgood scoring one and Hutchinson two.

An attacking unit with the maverick David Webb in support from the back was born. One of Chelsea's brightest-ever periods was about to explode. And the brightest light was going to be the King.

"There was only one player better than me and that was George Best. And he was the best! I was talked about in the same breath as George Best and that was good enough for me." With George Graham, Ossie had played off the main striker. With Tommy Baldwin and Bobby Tambling he had been the main striker. Now, with Hutchinson, he played off the main one again. "I preferred playing off the big fella, Hutch. They couldn't match us. In 1970 I scored thirty-one goals and he scored twenty-two. They couldn't stop us.

"Dave paid £5,000 to non-League Cambridge for him, and frankly when I first saw Hutch I thought it was about £4,995 too much! But he was awesome! He came here at twenty-two and packed up at twenty-seven. He broke every bone in his body! I wouldn't have swapped him for anybody. To play up front with him, and with Charlie Cooke, Huddy and Peter Houseman knocking balls in, they couldn't stop us.

"Huddy and Charlie together were fantastic. The only thing Charlie couldn't do was score goals. Apart from that he could do everything. He could dribble, he could run, he was quick, he had a great engine on him. Huddy could change a game. He could knock a ball in and they'd say: 'Cor, look at that, Ossie's made five yards!' But it wasn't the five yards I'd made, it was the quickness of the ball and the vision of Huddy.

"They were two great players together, and don't forget

Johnny Hollins, the work horse, the best engine I've ever seen in a footballer. Then there was that lovely lad Peter Houseman on the left, killed in a car accident aged thirty-two."

Here was a unit on the pitch, and a unit off it. Hutchinson quickly became Osgood's best friend. He became best man at his weddings! And as for Hudson...well, they all liked a drink!

Hudson had grown up and was still living across the road from Stamford Bridge. Age, or lack of it, was no barrier. "He showed me the drinking dens up and down the King's Road that I may have missed so far. We shared the same attitude to football, authority, drink and women."

The electric pace of his first season had gone. The year out through injury had changed him so much. But the adapted Osgood remained an outstanding player. "It made me a wiser player. You have a yard, but in the brain. You take people where they don't want to go, take them out and then back in. Over five or six yards I could take somebody on and they wouldn't catch me, and that's all I needed to score a goal."

The team stormed up the table, finishing in the top three for only the fourth time in the club's history. And they won the FA Cup for the first time. Osgood made history that still stands today.

In the third round they beat Birmingham City 3-0 at home and he scored one. In the fourth round they drew 2-2 with Burnley when he scored, then won the replay 3-1 away. In the fifth round he scored in the 4-1 win at Crystal Palace, and in the quarter-final he hit a hat-trick in the 4-2 win at Queens Park Rangers.

He put Chelsea back ahead in the 5-1 semi-final win over Watford, and then famously scored the equaliser in the victorious replay Cup Final win over Leeds. He scored in every round. "Only about five did it before me. Jeff Astle did it in 1968 for West Bromwich Albion." No-one has done it since. He was confident before he died that his record would stand for a long time. "The reason it's lasted so long is rotation now," he laughed.

The final said all there was to say about Osgood. His performance at Wembley was dreadful. He admitted it. His performance in the replay at Old Trafford was regal. His goal was his favourite ever. It was thousands of Chelsea fans' favourite ever. The team was so very special.

"We played QPR at Loftus Road and won 4-2 on a mud heap. We went to White Hart Lane on a terrible pitch and beat Watford 5-1. Okay, they were Third Division and we should beat them. But then we went to Wembley and thought we'd get a billiard table, but all of a sudden it was the Horse Show two weeks before, and it was sand everywhere. It was terrible, like playing on a beach, and we scored two goals. Eleven goals in three games!"

Finalists Leeds, of course, were the best, the hardest and nastiest team in the country. Chelsea were the opposite…or that was the image. "We were the flair players. We could turn it on. We couldn't turn it on every week, but when we did we were awesome.

"You had to have bottle, you had to have class, you had to have steel. Leeds at that time were one of the best sides in the world, eleven internationals on the pitch and one, Paul Madeley, sitting on the bench. They were bullies, Leeds, but they couldn't bully our boys. Chopper (Ron Harris), Webby (David Webb), (John) Dempsey, (Eddie) McCreadie, you couldn't bully them. And behind them, the Cat in goal!"

At Wembley, Chelsea equalised twice. After extra time it was 2-2. At Old Trafford, Leeds led for much of the game. "The replay was an epic, an absolute battle. There was so much bad feeling. I just remember swapping passes and then Charlie floating it in there, and it was like slow motion. I couldn't believe it. I had so much time."

He dived, he headed, he scored. He jumped up, and then

emotion took over, and he dropped his head and raised shaking fists to the Chelsea fans. It was 1-1 and this was going to be Chelsea's Cup. Charlie Cooke laughs about it now. "Ossie made the most of it as he always did. I've got to admit it was a great ball I gave him, I floated it perfectly, and I couldn't believe it when he dived. He never dived to head the ball. He crashed it home, it was such a great header, and he put his fists up in the air to the fans behind the goal, and that was Ossie. He got the most out of all the moments. He really gave the fans great moments. There he was, raising the fans and raising us at the same time."

Osgood's crown was firmly in place. David Webb got the winner and Chelsea held on. "When you think of the tackles that went in that day!" Ossie laughed. "Eddie McCreadie kicked Billy Bremner in the head in the penalty area and it wasn't even a free-kick! I put myself about, on the field and off it! We knew we could match them."

That, of course, was the truth. Osgood now was hard, strong, he could explode in temper as much as in brilliance, he could take on the dirtiest of centre-halves in the dirtiest of times, and still find the space for his brilliance to make the difference. "To win the FA Cup was very, very important to us. The fans had never won it and it was absolutely brilliant to do it for them. We came back to Euston and to see the Chelsea Pensioners crying, it was fantastic."

The party culture was now in full gear. That February he had finally made his England debut with the media long demanding his call-up. A 3-1 win in Belgium was followed by a heavy drinking night out in Brussels with legends Bobby Moore and Alan Ball. There were two substitute appearances in the World Cup in 1970, but he was never properly called upon by Sir Alf Ramsay and he was never trusted by the England manager, who required working-class players above world-class ones.

The next season didn't start as well, and the off-pitch headlines were more regular now. Trouble always seemed to be looming. Osgood's insistence on looking after himself on the pitch since his broken leg was getting him into more trouble. In the end the FA called him in and in January 1971 he found himself banned for a ridiculous eight weeks. Bans at this time were rare and time-orientated rather than for matches. He hadn't been sent off. You didn't get sent off in these days.

Chelsea were in the quarter-finals of the European Cup Winners' Cup, but already out of the FA and League Cups and not challenging for the title. "I knew I was being made an example of because Chelsea's reputation as hard drinking playboys was beginning to niggle in high places, as well as causing Dave Sexton some embarrassment and annoyance."

He missed ten games during which Hutchinson suffered a broken leg and Chelsea lost 2-0 in Bruges in the European quarter-final first leg. He returned to the team for the second leg. Another great European night was in the making. With nine minutes left and Chelsea leading 1-0 – 2-1 down on aggregate – the King scored, and in extra time he scored again and went to his people. "I was so elated that I was back and we were through that I carried on running, jumped the dog track and fell to my knees and saluted the human cauldron that was the Shed. It was a special moment in my life."

Chelsea won 4-0, and progressed to the Final. But he had picked up a knee ligament injury and was struggling. For the Final, against Real Madrid in Athens, he had cortisone injections. These were painful but for big-time players were thought part of the job. In years to come the hangover from them would near cripple a number of players, and Osgood was one. Indeed, he needed a new knee early in the 2000s.

The Final turned into another epic. He scored, of course. Madrid equalised in the last minute. He had to come off as the injection wore off, but Chelsea lasted out in extra time, and in the day between the game and the replay he joined Cooke and Baldwin for a long drinking session at a hotel.

Come the Friday, hangover finally lifted, injection to the knee received, he went out and scored another great goal. "Tommy laid a ball in my path, I let rip from about 25 yards and the ball just seared into the net." That made it 2-0. Chelsea won 2-1 and brought a European trophy home to the Fulham Road on an open-top double-decker bus, the second consecutive season of such a parade. Osgood wasn't just the King of Stamford Bridge, he was becoming the King of Europe.

Two games into the following season Sexton transfer-listed Osgood. Hutchinson had re-broken his leg in training, Chelsea had lost 3-2 at home to Manchester United and an emotional Sexton felt Osgood's attitude, even though he had scored, wasn't the same as Hutchinson's. Their brittle relationship started to disintegrate.

Immediately there were demonstrations by fans and not long afterwards Sexton withdrew the listing. The King seemed bigger than the coach.

Chelsea bobbled along in that 1971-72 season. Osgood was back to being the main targetman, playing mostly next to Baldwin and later also new signing Chris Garland, both quite small forwards. Another new signing, midfielder Steve Kember, was difficult to fit into the team, and there was growing unrest with the manager.

"Dave was another Tinkerman," Osgood said, referring to Chelsea's manager at the time he was talking, Claudio Ranieri. "Huddy was one of the best midfield players Chelsea had ever had, and Dave started playing him on the wing."

His eight goals in two legs against Luxembourg team Jeunesse Hautcharage boosted his goal tally and his profile. It was a European goalscoring record. Chelsea won the first leg

8-0 – he got a hat-trick – and he publicly bet Bonetti £20 that he would score six in the return. He got five!

He scored eighteen League goals that season, so he had a good year, but it turned into a frustrating one. After the European goalfest, Chelsea were eliminated from the Cup Winners' Cup by Swedish part-timers Atvidaberg. The team never challenged for the Championship, but reached the final of the League Cup. A third Cup Final in three years! The balloon was still full of air.

The semi-final was won over two legs against Tottenham. Osgood scored the opening goal at Stamford Bridge with typical cheek. John Pratt was shielding the ball back to goalkeeper Jennings, and just before it got there Osgood nudged Pratt in the back and he went crashing into the goalkeeper. Osgood angled the loose ball into the net and strode off in celebration and laughter.

Scoring goals past Pat Jennings
From near and from far.

The week before the Final, Chelsea's season suffered a major blow. In the FA Cup fifth round, Osgood and Webb put Chelsea two-up at Second Division Orient, but in the last twenty-five minutes the small East London outfit scored three. The flair players seemed languid, disinterested. Now the whole season rested on success at Wembley.

The League Cup Final was against Stoke City, who were an old team. Their club had never won a major honour. They took the lead. Just before half-time, Osgood equalised, his first Wembley goal. He knocked it in with his right boot while lying on the ground after a mêlée. The King ruled! "We played so well at Wembley," he lamented. Garland enjoyed his best Chelsea game. Cooke had a fine second half, and with Hudson dominated midfield. But it wasn't to be, and Stoke won 2-1.

The first real cracks in the side were visible. The showbiz lifestyle seemed to be all-important. In his autobiography, he admitted: 'A police car chase involving Tommy Baldwin in which a vodka bottle was thrown out from a car window seemed to encapsulate how wild we had become. Luckily, the bottle didn't hit Tommy.' Ossie didn't actually write who threw it. You'd only need one guess!

He finished the 1971-72 season with 31 goals again. But the following year things really deteriorated. The team finished twelfth, its lowest position since promotion in 1963. It got knocked out of the FA Cup in a sixth-round replay at Arsenal, and of the League Cup in a semi-final with Norwich City. At home to Arsenal Osgood volleyed the goal which was BBC *Match Of The Day's* Goal of the Season. He, at least, was still King.

Film star, screen babe Raquel Welch was brought to one home game and left before the end having downed a significant amount of brandy in the directors' seats, parading along the touchline the length of the pitch in front of the gap where the newly-developing East Stand was a building site. She knew Ossie was the King. She stopped in his line and blew him kisses. In a wonderfully professional moment he ignored her.

Bill Garner had been signed to try and replace Hutchinson, which didn't sit well with the close trio of Osgood, Baldwin and Hutchinson. Suddenly, a new generation of youngsters was coming into the team: Gary Locke, Graham Wilkins, Ian Britton, Mike Brolly. Osgood, quite remarkably, responded well and became a sort of father figure. In fact, he finished up winning the fans' Player of the Year for the only time.

"I loved the lads who were coming in," he said enthusiastically. "I remembered the way I was treated. And I think if you talk to Graham Wilkins, Ian Britton, Tommy Langley, Ray Wilkins and all those lads, they knew I loved them. They weren't good enough to take our place at that time, but they were good enough to come through. So why not nurture them and say carry on where we left off."

Graham Wilkins confirms his belief. "We all looked up to him," he says now. "He was the superstar. He was a father figure. He was so generous. When me and my missus had our first child, he must have bought Mothercare for us. He was so, so generous.

"When I first broke into the side he was still brilliant. As a targetman he was fantastic. It was like playing a ball off a brick wall, you knew where it was going to go and you'd get it back. He was a great header of the ball as well. And he was nasty when he had to be! He could look after himself.

"And he'd look after us youngsters. I remember Mike Summerbee spitting at me once, I was only seventeen, and Ossie had a right go at him!"

Things, however, got even worse the following season. On Boxing Day Chelsea lost 4-2 at home to West Ham, having led 2-0. On December 29th they lost 1-0 at home to Liverpool. The rumours were that Osgood and Hudson weren't in the best state of health. On January 1st 1974, Sexton dropped Osgood, Hudson, Baldwin and also Bonetti. Chelsea won 2-1 at Sheffield United with goals from Hollins and Kember.

Osgood and Hudson were transfer-listed again, and in February were sold for a lot of money. The club was in massive debt because of the East Stand. Hudson couldn't stand Sexton, but with Osgood the relationship had been more complex.

"Dave lost faith in us. He panicked. There was no way I wanted to leave the club. Dave said I asked for a transfer, and I still say to this day that I didn't. Huddy did, I didn't. And then we were told that Dave had got the sack! Eddie McCreadie rang for us to come down the King's Road and he got the champagne out. But they re-instated him and that was me on my bike then. I was gone!"

What a mess! Sexton was sacked and re-instated, or the wrong publicity had gone out. Hudson went to Stoke and led them to being runners-up in the title race, their best-ever season. Osgood went to Southampton and won the FA Cup again. Chelsea finished seventeenth in 1974 and, after Sexton was finally sacked early the following season, were relegated in 1975.

When Chelsea were back in the top flight but still in disarray in 1978, he returned, brought home by Danny Blanchflower. But the legs had gone altogether. He scored on his first appearance, of course, but his opening goal was wasted in a 7-2 defeat at Middlesbrough. He played centre-half to try and help out in an FA Cup tie at Manchester United. Chelsea got relegated again. He left for the last time as a player.

In 1983 Hudson went back too. He didn't play and moved on to Stoke again, but the pull of Chelsea and those King's Road boys – Charlie Cooke had gone and returned before Osgood – to the club was irresistible.

Throughout the years of Ken Bates' chairmanship, 1982-2003, his relationship with Osgood was a love-hate one. Sometimes Osgood was welcome at Stamford Bridge, sometimes he wasn't. When Bates invited him back to be host to the sponsors, he was ecstatic. But it was always going to be a short story.

By now he was successful on the after-dinner circuit and with golf weekends. He was living successfully as the King. But when his closest friend, the great Ian Hutchinson, died and Bates made derogatory remarks about him, the 'hate' side of their relationship re-surfaced, and Osgood went to the papers. He was sacked from the hospitality work again.

He'd keep in touch with Chelsea people. He used to ring me regularly to find out what was going on at his club. Fans like

Mick Crossan would make sure he was at the games. He'd even travel to Europe as a private guest of a group of fans and make some money for being the King.

What he delighted in almost more than anything else was the arrival and longevity at the club of Gianfranco Zola. He saw his soul alive and playing. He was always willing to hand his crown over to the player he referred to as 'the little man'. And Zola, being Zola, always treated Osgood with the greatest respect and always gave him the time of day. On such occasions Osgood was a man, a fan, and a King in heaven.

As soon as Roman Abramovich took over the club, he was back doing the job he loved most, hosting the sponsors on a matchday. "I will never be different," he proclaimed. "I will never stop being a Chelsea supporter. I never will."

On March 1st 2006 he was attending the funeral of a family member when almost without warning his heart stopped beating. He was probably dead by the time he had fallen to the ground. He was 59-years-old. At the next home game, almost perfectly against Tottenham and won with a last minute William Gallas goal, his old team-mates collected at Stamford Bridge, and his life was celebrated with a minute's applause around a special wreath before the game. Outside, a massive shrine had developed, flowers, scarves, shirts, photographs, messages. Amongst them, perhaps most heart-felt of all, was a photograph placed by his former team-mate John Boyle, of John's wedding with Osgood as best man.

On October 1st 2006 a memorial service was held at the ground. The Shed End was opened to supporters. His ashes were laid, in an urn, deep below the penalty spot. A plaque was unveiled behind the goal in front of the seats.

On June 1st 2007 I attended a supporters' dinner in Milton Keynes. I sat with the guests of honour, Lynn Osgood and Hutchinson's partner of several years Elaine Thatcher. Lynne and Elaine had long been the closest of friends and, when

Ossie had married Lynn soon after retiring, Hutch had the opportunity of meeting Elaine. The Osgood-Hutchinson partnership was alive, vibrant and as good a pairing as ever. The boys would have been proud and delighted.

At every Chelsea game, his song still rings out. He represents the modern history of Chelsea: outrageously talented, full of swagger, loves a good time, not always responsible for his actions, a loveable rogue – a King.

And out from the Shed
There rose a young star
Scoring goals past Pat Jennings
From near and from far.
And Chelsea won
Like we all knew they would
And the star of that great team
Was Peter Osgood.

Osgood, Osgood, Osgood, Osgood,
Born is the King of Stamford Bridge.

Osgood, Osgood, Osgood, Osgood,
Born is the King of Stamford Bridge.

Players who have scored in every round of the FA Cup

Archie Hunter	Aston Villa	1887
Sandy Brown	Tottenham Hotspur	1901
Harry Hampton	Aston Villa	1905
Harold Blackmore	Bolton Wanderers	1929
Ellis Rimmer	Sheffield Wednesday	1935
Frank O'Donnell	Preston North End	1937
Stan Mortensen	Blackpool	1948
Jackie Milburn	Newcastle United	1951
Nat Lofthouse	Bolton Wanderers	1953
Charlie Wayman	Preston North End	1954
Jeff Astle	West Bromwich Albion	1968
Peter Osgood	Chelsea	1970

The romantic who dribbled to glory

Charlie Cooke

Go back in time: Joe Cole, Gianfranco Zola, Pat Nevin, Charlie Cooke...great dribblers, world-class ball manipulators, visionaries, fantasists. Entertainers!

Perhaps the one incident Charlie Cooke is best remembered for now is his perfectly gorgeous chip to set up Peter Osgood's diving-headed equaliser in the 1970 FA Cup Final Replay. It is ironic but not coincidence that the master dribbler should be recalled for a pass, that the man who is still uneasy that he was stuck out on the wing for so much of his Chelsea career should be revered for a piece of central midfield finesse.

Of course, if you were there, through the second half of the 1960s and much of the 1970s, there were those jinks, drag-backs, flicks, feints, accelerations; there were those runs past one, two, three and sometimes four, five, six opponents. No wonder he was loved. But there was never any doubt that he could play, he could pass, he could unlock defences in several ways. He had so much to his game.

People recall the 1970s team by saying Osgood, Cooke and Hudson, and those three were the outstanding attacking players. Osgood so often scored in the big games. Cooke so often delivered in them.

He had and retains an anti-tactical love of the game. Learn the skills, practice the skills; beat the opponent, win the match. Be the best! It was a time when football was as entertaining as it has ever been, and it was an era when off the pitch the young were taking over the world. Many of them were doing it from London. It was the time of The Beatles, King's Road, the death of the minimum wage for footballers – it was a time to party.

There was a period later when it wasn't as easy for old players to go back to Chelsea as it is now, and Charlie has enjoyed his renewed relationship with the club in recent years. He is the Cincinnati Kid. He's lived in Cincinnati, USA, for 15 years or so, and his enthusiasm for the teaching and learning of skills remains of child-like enthusiasm. His joy at how his skills are remembered now has been a surprise to him.

"Often I don't get here for long periods", he said on one visit, "but then it does my heart good to hear people talk about those times and some of the games that even I can't remember. It does this old guy's heart a lot of good. It was a crazy, fun world for all the players. I think we got through relatively unscathed. It was an exciting world, on the field there were a lot of exciting players, a lot of exciting games, an exciting team, and you wouldn't change it for the world.

"A lot of things you might change in your own behaviour perhaps, but the whole experience I wouldn't change now."

In 1971, after Chelsea had drawn the European Cup Winners' Cup Final and a replay was to be staged two days later, Real Madrid's star attacker Amancio said: "If we stop Cooke, we will win." They didn't. He was majestic. Chelsea won!

In the day in between the games Charlie got hammered drinking in an Athens bar with Tommy Baldwin and Osgood. He has done well to come through unscathed.

In September 1968 Chelsea drew 1-1 with West Ham United, and Charlie Cooke went on one of those legendary dribbles.

He kept feigning to strike the ball and jinking beyond the next challenge. The sequence became central to the titles of ITV's *The Big Match*, the Sunday afternoon counter to Saturday night's *Match Of The Day*.

Cooke feels strongly about two things these days that would, and should have made his career even better. He should have played more in central midfield, and he should have scored more goals.

"See, I missed the goal. I went through four, five or six, and then missed the goal!" He scolds himself.

In fact, at the last moment he decided not to shoot and tried to cross on to an arriving head, but the ball drifted away.

"I did the same at Aberdeen once, went past five or six and put it over the bar. This is one of the things I've always regretted. When I started out as a 16, 17-year-old, for the first few years of my career I think I was second top scorer in the team. But when you keep reading press reports and hear people saying you're a chance creator, you're the guy who makes things for other people, you take on that persona. And so I started thinking that I didn't care about scoring goals. If you can make a couple of chances for other people, or if you can make a couple of goals, that's a sign of a really good player. Whereas if you're the one who puts it in, that's okay but it's no big deal.

"Now when I look back, I think God! That's the one thing I lacked, I didn't score enough. I had a good strike with both feet. And that's how deeply ingrained it was when I got to the penalty area against West Ham. I'd beaten those people and been happy with that. That was me. Always happy to beat people but always happy to let someone else finish."

There's a story, maybe myth, maybe true, that when manager Tommy Docherty introduced Charlie Cooke to the Chelsea dressing room for the first time that Terry Venables said he had a reputation of being super-skilful and threw the ball hard at him, without warning, to find out. Cooke controlled it with aplomb and performed a trick or two before jettisoning it back.

You have to picture this dressing room. Docherty had built his team of 'Docherty's Diamonds' and then all but destroyed them. A year earlier when they were just failing to land a treble, he sent eight players home in disgrace after they had broken a random curfew in Blackpool, and the scar was still open. A less impressive domestic season had followed, but a wonderful European campaign, the club's first great year in overseas competition, was climaxing in the semi-final of the old Inter-Cities Fairs Cup. There had been a 2-0 defeat at Barcelona. Cooke had been signed for a then club record £72,500 in time to play the second leg.

He was clearly set to replace Venables in midfield. Venables had once been captain and was always the leader of Docherty's Diamonds, but the two had fallen out. Cooke cannot confirm the story. But there is much of the 1960s and 1970s he cannot confirm. The old adage, if you remember the 1960s you weren't there, is so true of him. He was there! He doesn't remember a lot of it.

"I have a tough time remembering that, I have to be honest," he says with a smile. He talks in a half-American, half-Scottish soft brogue. "But when everyone mentions it, I say, 'oh yeah, that happened.' But to tell you the truth, I don't remember it. I'll take the applause and say that happened, but I don't remember that it did!"

Venables may not have appreciated Docherty, but Cooke did. "Tommy Doc had a way around him, he was never awkward around people. He was always a great fan of mine. He didn't go out of his way to make me feel at home, he was just a natural."

But it wasn't easy for the new boy, who wanted to take the world on in a dribbling fest. Barry Bridges, England centre-forward, had just walked out, Venables was sidelined, Peter Bonetti had made it clear he wanted away, and the dressing room was falling apart. Chelsea beat Barcelona 2-0 with two own goals, but in a play-off – no penalty shoot-outs in those days – lost 5-0 back in Spain when one or two players had reportedly decided it was the end of the season and a few drinks should be part of the pre-match preparation.

"That was bizarre," says Charlie. "It didn't go well that night. I can't remember the details, just the feeling after the game of tremendous disappointment at getting a drubbing. There were all the dressing room problems, some of the players were about to leave, some knew already they were leaving, there was not a good feeling about the whole situation. It was a disappointing start but it didn't discolour anything that was to come."

And what was to come was sheer entertainment. In his recent autobiography, *The Bonnie Prince*, Charlie celebrates that style. Venables had later described the new team as "individualistic", and Charlie likes that. "I doubt Terry will read any apologies from Osgood, McCreadie, Hollins, Alan Hudson, David Webb or any of the other players who might have symbolised that individualism, and he certainly won't hear any from me. That's who we were, and I'm thankful for it and for the fact that we weren't swallowed up in the coaching twaddle of the day back then.

"I'm thankful Chelsea were the kind of team they were. We may have underachieved – perhaps that's a book in itself – and heaven knows we've got plenty to answer for, but I wouldn't have changed our style one iota, even if I could have."

Splendid autobiography. Read it!

Strangely, having arrived at Chelsea at the end of the 1965-66 season, Cooke stayed in London for the summer. "It was just going into the 1966 World Cup. I stayed for a little bit and saw most of the World Cup. It was strange. I was in digs."

He believes that helped him settle into his new environment. With McCreadie, George Graham and John Boyle all in the team, he had plenty of Scots to mix with.

Come his League debut in the first game of the following season, he scored the winner at West Ham United. This, remember, was the West Ham with the World Cup-winning trio of Bobby Moore, Geoff Hurst and Martin Peters. And what a winner! "I saw that goal recently in black and white footage! It was a good goal! I collected the ball 10, 15 yards over the halfway line, went all the way to the edge of the box, kind of faked Bobby Moore, it wasn't a fake so much as just getting enough space to shoot, and scored with my left foot from outside the box."

He believes his summer had helped prepare him. "That goal at West Ham was a nice start, all the things came together for a good start. Tommy Doc always used me as a midfield player."

After ten games Chelsea were top of the table. Bobby Tambling was scoring goals for fun, Peter Osgood was the best teenager in the First Division and, although Graham had now joined the exodus, Baldwin had arrived as a replacement and was already scoring. Next game, however, Osgood suffered a broken leg, and the team fell away. The dressing room problem wouldn't die. "There was a lot of stuff left over from the Blackpool incident. People like Johnny Hollins couldn't get on with Tommy Doc after that. Eddie Mac...there was a definite hangover."

Cooke's performances were patchy. Maybe settling wasn't as easy as he thought. A typical Chelsea passage saw a 5-5 home draw with West Ham followed two weeks later after two 2-1 defeats by a 6-1 caning at Sheffield Wednesday (admittedly in Bonetti's absence), followed one week later by a 4-1 home win over Southampton. Cooke finds it as perplexing now as then. "I had a terrific game at home in the

Southampton game, I remember the match reports. I remember the West Ham game, we couldn't believe we'd lost five goals. We thought we deserved the five goals we got. But it wasn't an easy time."

In those days the FA Cup was as important as the League. Chelsea had won the League in 1955, but never the FA Cup. In fact, in over 60 years since the club's formation, the final had been reached only once and never a Wembley showpiece. In 1965 and '66, the two years before Cooke's arrival, there had been semi-final heartache. Favourites Chelsea had lost to Liverpool and then Sheffield Wednesday, both at Villa Park.

Now in 1967, with League form poor, Cooke's Chelsea reached a third successive semi-final, and the opposition was powerful Leeds United. Leeds were the favourites. Chelsea won 1-0. Cooke made the goal for Osgood's expensive and not too successful replacement, Tony Hateley. But the game is more remembered for Leeds' late disallowed goal when Peter Lorimer's free-kick had to be retaken.

"Getting to the final was a massive relief," Charlie says, almost reliving the sigh! "It was going to a tie, it was highly competitive. I got the ball and made the cross..." it was from the left-wing having cut in to his right foot, "...it was a nice cross, and Tony Hateley headed in. It was a nice goal.

"But then the Peter Lorimer goal was disallowed, and there was so much made of Chelsea having cheated Leeds. We never felt Leeds were cheated. It was a great story to continue the Chelsea-Leeds rivalry, but we never felt they were cheated. We deserved that goal. That was an example of how we produced in big games."

Sadly, Chelsea's first Wembley FA Cup Final was not one of those games. Tottenham won 2-1. "I always look back on that as a fantastic disappointment. We got there and then we played like dummies. I thought we were terrible. Spurs deserved to win it, and I can't remember us creating much at all, just giving the ball away all the time.

"Sometimes folk would give their right arm just to get there, but we felt ever so disappointed."

There was to be more disappointment for him at the beginning of the following season. After a few games, Tommy Docherty was sacked. Dave Sexton succeeded him, and his football life was to change.

Charlie Cooke likes to enjoy himself. He answered the phone to talk for this chapter while fishing in California. He has always liked to enjoy himself. Most importantly, he's liked to enjoy himself on the football pitch.

For many years now he has been running soccer schools based on the Coerver coaching method which is all about skill, fun, improving ability, winning your personal battles on the pitch – it's about enjoying being as good as you can. He's helped take the schools all over the world.

That was the football environment which Tommy Docherty welcomed him into at Chelsea. Dave Sexton brought a more scientific environment, a coaching manual, a thinking mind. But with Osgood back in the side, and Hudson soon to come, and with maverick defenders like McCreadie and new signing David Webb, the exuberance of expressing yourself remained the greatest quality of the team.

"Our game was a little bit more off the cuff than now," Charlie says. "But there was a lot of macho play between the teams. The players today are great athletes, perhaps there's more skill, more culture, but there isn't the same vibrance or life about it as then."

Sexton had some problems to sort out. The team was shipping goals. Osgood wasn't scoring. He clearly didn't think Cooke was the answer to the gap left by Venables. Soon, Cooke was pushed wide to the wing and Osgood withdrawn to midfield. Cooke did brilliantly wide, and his central midfield days became rare. Ironically, however, they were to include the victorious FA Cup Final and European Cup Winners' Cup Final replays.

"I felt very strong and able to cover a lot of ground in midfield. I always liked to be in the middle of the field, you get more of the ball, more in the game, you're not out there kind of scratching your backside wondering when you're going to get the ball, and you don't have full-backs screaming down your neck and then you have to get back to cover for them. I certainly preferred the middle of the field.

"I pulled a lot of punches when it came to Dave. I don't think he thought of me as a top player, he thought I held the ball too long. He was an England coach and talked about as a great strategist. But it was all about show a diagram with four defenders across the field, make an area behind them and shade it, and say put the ball in there. That's football by numbers to me.

"So I played wide because that was where he put me. I was brought up to tow the line and get on with it. I let myself down by not saying enough. And I showed an ability on the wing which Dave used because he didn't have other players to take up that role."

Within a few weeks of Sexton taking over, he suggested to Cooke that he go and talk to John Harris, manager of Sheffield United about a move. Cooke was shocked. He couldn't see why he wasn't wanted. He refused. Not long later Chelsea bought Alan Birchenall from the same team, and suddenly he registered that he would have been part of the deal.

Birchenall was an honest, hard running, strong, tireless forward. He wasn't skilful. It wasn't the Chelsea Cooke had become accustomed to. But he stayed and flourished on the wing, he took full-backs on, he took anyone on who covered, he cut in, he crossed, he penetrated, he set up goals, he scored a few, and he finished up winning Chelsea's Player of the Year award. One in the eye for Sexton, he thought!

"How sweet that was! I felt in my whole career under Dave that if one was to go, it was me. I think it was part of the reason he played me wide, because I was disposable."

He also starred for Scotland against world champions England in a 1-1 draw at Hampden Park. "That was a time when I was flying in my life and in my career.

"But I remember (England manager) Alf Ramsay making quite a lot after the game of my holding the ball and beating people, and that helped England. I thought: **** you! That seemed to symbolise the Dave Sexton and England attitude to the game.

"I was in Cyprus after that, staying in the same hotel as Alf Ramsay that summer, and he never acknowledged me! I just thought: **** you!

"Scotland were unlucky not to win that game, and I had a good game! For him to say what he said was just uncharitable."

Charlie Cooke was not your average footballer either on or off the field. He was a thinker and a drinker off it! He used to talk about the art of positive thinking. Later he conducted interviews for the *London Evening News* with people like Prime Minister Edward Heath. But all the time there was the wildness of the 'swinging sixties' years cascading through the days and nights.

Sometimes, you wondered about his thinking. Sometimes, after three or four blinding consecutive games, he seemed to think himself out of form – as if he couldn't possibly produce another performance of such quality.

He denies this. "The League's always been high quality, so no matter who you are, even if you're a Pele, you're going to have quiet games. Some teams you got to grips with, there wasn't a lot of cover for the full-backs, but others you had to get the ball deeper in midfield, there'd be three or four covering the full-back, you'd have much quieter games.

"Some games were set up for you to be a star! I used to try hard enough. But I didn't rely on simply being a star."

In some games, he seemed to take a dislike to an opponent, and if Chelsea were winning he'd beat him going forward, turn and come back round him, then beat him again. He denies this too.

"There's no question I overdid it sometimes. But I used to pride myself on being a good professional. When we had a good day on our hands, if we got in front we could go on and win. I remember sometimes when opponents were lippy and telling you they were going to break your leg and all that bull, I was happy to have them on toast. I didn't like the bulls***. I didn't talk on the pitch.

"So if they gave some really demeaning lip and I had the chance to over-indulge, maybe. But I took pride on being a good pro. Get your job done and shut up!

"We were always up there at the top challenging, but always fell away towards the end of the season. I think it was something to do with youth and a little bit of London wildness and craziness. There was a great spirit in the dressing room, a lot of hard competitors: Chopper Harris, Eddie McCreadie, Ossie up front could give it and take it, it was a good, exciting mix of players. But I think all would hold their hands up and say we should have done better."

He couldn't have done better on an icy day in late December 1969. By now Chelsea were really buzzing. Hudson, 18-years-old, had established himself next to Hollins in midfield, Osgood was scoring sublimely up again in attack and, next to Osgood, Ian Hutchinson had been bought, the powerful, influential presence that Birchenall never quite achieved.

The second game in two days – a 2-1 home win over

Southampton had been enjoyed on Boxing Day – was at Crystal Palace. The pitch was a skating rink. Chelsea won 5-1. Osgood scored four, Peter Houseman the other. Cooke ran the game and was unstoppable. Unbelievably, on a day when a player hit four goals, Cooke was unarguably man of the match. He skated – others slipped.

"It was one of those games you dream of," he recalls. "If things went well I used to make excuses. Ah, I had nails in my studs so I'd get a better grip! I never gave myself credit when it went well. Looking back now, I'll take the credit!"

So sometimes it was great, indeed often it was great, but other times...well, it was good old Chelsea. Charlie's closest friend in those days was Tommy Baldwin.

"It was like a good roller-coaster ride," laughs Tommy, still close to Charlie across the Atlantic and still getting together with him at every possible opportunity. "We were up there one minute and down the next.

"Charlie was a great fella, a great pal to me. We were room-mates, we both lived in Fulham in the late sixties and early seventies, so we were virtually neighbours. We had a good social life, we were up King's Road all the time. Alan Hudson lived in Fulham, but all the other players lived outside. We just had such a great time. And the football was going well, we were in all those finals."

Cooke, Baldwin, Osgood, Hutchinson, Hudson, McCreadie and Boyle. Now that was some party for starters.

"There were some wild nights" Charlie admits. "You've got to remember, it was London, it was kind of the swinging sixties, a lot of things were going well for the whole country then. The economy was booming, I think the film industry was booming, and of course we were having a good time here at the club. There was great team spirit. Tommy Doc had started it off, Dave Sexton had come along, there was a lot of success on the field, and off the field it was fun from Monday to Friday.

"We had some embarrassing moments, some pretty crazy things we all regret a bit. I can remember one day – this is embarrassing – we were in for treatment, I think Tommy was there, Ossie was there, I'm not sure if Hutch was, Alan Hudson was there. It came to lunchtime and Harry Medhurst, the old physio, had dealt with all our injuries, and we had to come back at 1.30, two o'clock, and it was say 11.30 in the morning.

"So we said, 'let's go for lunch', and we went to the restaurant round the corner, I don't think it exists any longer with the new development, and it became a fun lunch. By the time we were due back we said we'd better get out of here, but it went on and it went on, and it got to 2.15, 2.30, and suddenly Dave Sexton arrived and said: 'What the hell are you guys doing here?'

"We were all embarrassed...well, half of us were too sozzled to be embarrassed. Then I can remember going back to the ground saying: 'Oh Christ, we're in trouble now!' And there was a little wall about this high (he holds his hand out at knee height) and I can remember we were walking along talking, thinking it was funny, and I remember toppling over it, lying on the ground, still speaking to the guys. And of course they were just as high as I was and having a laugh about it.

"It was a great laugh at the time, but it was pretty embarrassing. That week we were dropped I think, and rightly so!"

Baldwin thinks it was assistant-manager Ron Suart who turned up, not Sexton. But why in their state should two people remember details in the same way?

Yet despite this and similar stories, Cooke doesn't accept that this team was unmanageable. "There was a great team spirit, so we always did it together. I wouldn't say we were unmanageable, but it needed a special kind of manager to do it. Dave had an inability to talk straight to people, and that helped cause frustration with Ossie and the guys, people like Boylers, Tommy Baldwin and myself."

But this wonderful, crazy, frustrating, entertaining team was about to hit glory like no Chelsea side had before.

In Chelsea's first 100 years the club never lost a Cup game to Leeds United or Real Madrid. In 1969-70, Chelsea played Leeds four times in knockout games. In 1970-71 they played Real Madrid twice. It was a time of glory. Charlie Cooke was at his peak.

The FA Cup had become the Holy Grail. The club was 65-years-old and hadn't won it. There had been nine previous semi-finals and two finals. The season didn't start well. Osgood was in central midfield for the first game at Anfield where Liverpool won 4-1. John Boyle, Peter Houseman and Cooke were all tried there over the next few weeks.

Leeds away was a tough League Cup tie, but Chelsea battled to a 1-1 draw and in the replay back at Stamford Bridge Cooke scored in a 2-0 win.

"We had a pretty good record against Leeds," he says, explaining their confidence whenever facing the most feared side in the land. "They were a fantastic team, but we held our own. We had a couple of excellent results against them."

Hudson had been brought in for that game, and before the end of the year a unit was found that was sublime: Cooke, Hudson, Hollins, Houseman. Cooke dribbled, penetrated, created; Hollins powered, motored, scored long-range goals; Hudson dominated, linked, created; Houseman worked, crossed, crossed again, and scored a few.

The team rocketed up the First Division to finish third, and in the FA Cup beat Birmingham City 3-0, Burnley 3-1 away in a replay, Crystal Palace 4-1 away, Queens Park Rangers 4-2 away, and Watford 5-1 in the semi-final. This was as good as it gets.

Leeds awaited in the Final. Ten days beforehand, Hudson was injured. Who would play central midfield? Sexton chose Houseman, switched Cooke to the left and brought Baldwin in on the right. The pitch at Wembley was a disgrace. Chelsea got hammered but Bonetti was inspired. It was 2-2 at full time. For extra time Sexton switched Cooke and Houseman. Cooke was back in central midfield. In the replay eighteen days later, he was there for all two hours of normal and extra time.

"On the field it was sodden. The first goal Leeds got, Eddie Mac swung at it – we always kidded Eddie about his eyesight – but the ball didn't bounce. That was a very difficult field. It was an exciting game for Leeds because they were attacking all the time, but for the players it was a strength-sapping game. You couldn't get a lot going the way you wanted.

"Nobby (Peter Houseman) in the middle wasn't a natural there from my perspective. He was a wide-man. He wasn't the guy who would come blazing through and create something. Holly (John Hollins) and me was a good blend. Holly was straight forward and I was creating something.

"The second game was pretty rough and ugly. I saw years later some film of it and I had to wake myself up and say it was like that. There were some crazy tackles, some wild stuff."

Leeds had led twice at Wembley and Chelsea had come back each time. Leeds led in the replay at Old Trafford too. Then it happened. They were attacking, Chelsea countered. Ian Hutchinson had the ball and let Cooke take over in the middle of the park. He was surging forward. He looked up and picked out Osgood with a divine chip. Osgood, who had scored in every round but not yet in the final, dived forward and met it with all the grace and power it deserved. One-all! Osgood and Cooke!

"It was a nice pass. It was one of those right on the dime, and there was Ossie and he made the most of it of course, he went full length and put the icing on the cake. I think it was the only time he ever dived for a header! He'd jump...but dive? Oh, it was a great goal!"

Chelsea finally took the lead in extra time through David Webb, and the artists – football artists, and the other variety who knew how to enjoy themselves – had shown more strength, resolve and ability to mix it than the beasts of Leeds in order to reach the Holy Grail. It was one of the proudest moments in Chelsea history.

Sexton's response was to go out and buy a right-winger, Keith Weller, who played in the position Cooke normally filled.

"Keith was having a good spell. He was a straight-ahead player, the kind Dave liked. Similar to Johnny Hollins. He got on the end of things. He was honest. It was the same when we signed Stevie Kember from Crystal Palace."

Kember seemed earmarked to replace Hudson. Chris Garland also arrived, maybe to replace Baldwin. Sexton may argue that he had all the ability he needed, and required other qualities but, considering what an entertaining team he put out every week, his buys were pretty one-dimensional: Birchenall (hard-running forward), Webb (no-nonsense defender), Dempsey (no-nonsense defender), Hutchinson (powerful forward), Mulligan (good right-back), Phillips (back-up goalkeeper), Droy (mountainous defender), Weller (hard-working wide-man), Garland (hard-running forward), Kember (up-and-down midfielder) and Garner (multi-storey forward) being the main ones.

There were some legends and heroes and exceptional footballers in there, and Chelsea has much to be grateful to Dave Sexton for, but the threads left by Docherty were crucial to his success.

Injuries to Hutchinson allowed the manager to develop different shapes in the team. The European Cup Winners' Cup became the focus of the season. There were good wins against Aris Thessalonika and CSKA Sofia, and then a memorable victory over Bruges when the team came from a 2-0 first-leg defeat to win 4-0 after extra time. Everyone was on fire. Manchester City, the holders, were beaten in the semi-final. And so to the final.

Sexton went with a 4-5-1 shape. So Weller and Houseman were wide, and Cooke was inside with Hollins and Hudson. Cooke was superb. But Real Madrid equalised Osgood's goal in the last minute, and were on top in extra time. Chelsea held out for the replay. Madrid striker Amancio said: "If we stop Cooke, we will win."

Charlie says: "I don't think he would have said that if he was talking about me as a winger. They had Pirri in midfield, a super player. We had to be better."

Typical Chelsea, some of the team didn't create conditions in which to be better.

"The day in between the final and the replay I went out with Tommy (Baldwin), and it was a pretty wild day. That was only because we were in Athens, we had nothing to do, nobody expected a replay, so what the heck do you do with yourself? And as usual we did the enjoyable things, but it worked out okay in the end. We played well enough."

Osgood joined them but Hudson, to his eternal credit, fell across them and declined. It was pretty much an all-day session of cocktails. But it was long rather than intense.

"Even when we were out having a good time, everyone was always pretty dedicated to the game itself. No-one avoided the work that had to be done. We put it on the line for each other on the field. People worked their butts off. When it had to be done, it got done."

Sexton had a problem. Hollins was injured. Most people thought he would move Boyle forward from right-back to midfield and bring in Mulligan, but he surprised everyone by selecting just Cooke and Hudson in central midfield and recalling Baldwin in attack to partner Osgood. It was back to 4-4-2, but with two ball-players in the middle of the park. Cooke revelled in the space. He ran the game.

"People sing my praises for that game, but I didn't think I or the team played particularly well. But we battled through and got the result. But again, when it mattered he put me in that position. I did well for him there."

Chelsea won 2-1 without extra time and raised their first European trophy. It felt like the team and Charlie Cooke were on top of the world.

Weller was sold early the following season. Chelsea stuttered along in the top half of the League, now rarely fulfilling the beautiful game style of the previous years, but reached the FA Cup quarter-final and League Cup Final. In successive weekends they lost both. The FA Cup was a disaster: 2-0 up at Second Division Orient, lost 3-2. The League Cup was an embarrassment: beaten 2-1 by Stoke City, who won their only major trophy to date.

Astonishingly, early the following season (1972-73) Cooke and Mulligan were sold to Crystal Palace. Both quickly regretted the move, but couldn't see the point in staying after Sexton had agreed a deal.

Cooke had only just scored in Chelsea's 1-1 draw at Arsenal. "Some of my goals were nice goals. It was a good goal at Arsenal. I remember scoring a cracking goal at Fulham. But I took the corners or stayed outside the box. I was just never in there. It was a terrible habit. I so wanted to make the goals. Guys who could beat players were top of my list, skilled players. I wanted to be a skilled player.

"People who have seen the film of the League Cup Final say we played pretty well. We were so over-confident, so embarrassed, ashamed, that I haven't seen it."

Once again he was one of Chelsea's finest on the day.

Garland had his best game and Osgood scored his customary goal, but it was Cooke who as ever on the big occasion took the game to the opposition.

At Palace he became anonymous. But at Palace he wasn't witness to Chelsea also becoming anonymous, and then implosive. Sexton fell out with Osgood and Hudson and sold them both. The great era was over. The team was tumbling down the table. He needed to do something drastic.

Without warning, he bought Cooke back. Eighteen months had passed. It was an extraordinary piece of business.

The master of the dribble, now nearly 32, remarked at the time: "The fans at Stamford Bridge have always loved me – they'd clap me just for standing up in a strong wind."

Sexton lasted only until early the following season, and in 1974-75 the FA Cup winners of five years before and European winners of four years before were relegated. Cooke was the only shining, battling light. He won his second Player of the Year award.

"Dave didn't say a lot when he bought me back. He said he was happy to have me here. He was in deep straights: Ossie had just gone, Huddy had just gone. I knew what had been going on but hadn't been following it closely. I knew he was under pressure.

"But when I first arrived in the 1960s there was a lot of turmoil, and this time there wasn't. The situation helped young guys like Ray Wilkins settle down. It was an emotional time for me. I'd come to the club as a young player with a lot of talent and had done pretty well, I'd gone, and now I'd come back because certain circumstances were forcing it. The club's financial situation was bad.

"I was still taking people on, still had a lot of running in me. I wouldn't say I felt an elder statesman, but I did feel I was doing something valuable."

Baldwin, Webb and Hollins left, Houseman too, Hutchinson

rarely played because of injury, Dempsey was the same. Only Bonetti and Harris from the great days were still around, and when former team-mate Eddie McCreadie became manager he fashioned a team for the 1976-77 season which left Harris and Cooke on the sidelines. Both came in towards the end of the season to help secure promotion.

Back in the top flight Charlie was mysteriously used as a centre-forward for a while by new manager Ken Shellito, but that didn't give him the impetus to score goals, and he decided to call it a day at the end of the year and made a new life in America.

There he played, then coached, then set up coaching schools. One morning after a customary heavy drinking session the night before, he suffered a severe headache. That evening he enjoyed another drinking session. The next morning the headache returned and was even worse. It was destructive.

He made a simple decision. He didn't want it again. He stopped drinking. Just like that! No religious insight, no detox, no battle with demons. He just didn't want that headache. That was the best part of 25 years ago. It's been no problem, he's never touched alcohol again. He loves being off the booze.

Whenever he's gone out on the Stamford Bridge pitch at half-time during games in the last few years, he's run out. He may be in his 60s, but on the pitch beneath the grey hairs he looks like a young man. He is still fit beyond belief.

Charlie Cooke may decry some of his achievements, he may always have had a self-destruct button too near to his centre of gravity, but he destroyed far more opponents than ever could deal with him. He was dashing! He was of his time. And he had the ability to be of any time.

"Chelsea was such a big part of my life. It was a big part of everyone's life. I was eleven years there. You know what? I think I deserved my Player of the Year awards. I'm proud of them now.

"It's only when I went back and wrote the book that I could tell you what Player of the Year awards I got. It used to be that tough Scottish thing, 'they don't mean anything to me,' but they make me very proud now.

"If you'd told me when I was playing that I'd go back and be selected for a Chelsea Team of the Century and that it would be important to me and I'd be proud of it, I'd have laughed you off the face of the earth. Now I'm so proud, I'm so tickled."

He laughs and decides to reveal one more truth. "When we were in the dressing room after games, you'd wash, you'd shower, the guys would do their hair and made sure they'd look great for the fans, but I used to think that was vanity. I never did that! I thought pride in the Player of the Year was vanity. Now looking back, I'm so proud.

"And the outcome of that is, I haven't got a good photo of myself! Scottish people are weird like that!"

Peter Osgood on tactics towards the end of the game
"When we were knackered we'd just pass it to Charlie and he'd keep it for five minutes and we'd have a rest."

Charlie Cooke when he returned to Chelsea after 18 months at Crystal Palace
"I hope they don't expect too much for 17 grand! I'm going to try and play the way I did in my two or three great seasons here. I know that's what the crowd want as well. Some people may doubt me coming back, but I believe I can live up to what is required and entertain the showbusiness element at Chelsea for four more years. I've got to. I've dropped money to come back!"

Tommy Baldwin on his friend Charlie Cooke

"He was a great footballer, one of the greatest. We may have been going up the King's Road everyday, but Charlie was a great trainer, he used to come back in the afternoon and work on his speed and things. He'd dribble and dribble but never shoot. He'd give it to me and that's how I got most of my goals. We'd walk a few in. He was an entertainer. You don't get many like that today. We used to call him the 'tanner ball player', but he was even better than that. He was strong, fit. Given the life he had he was as strong and fit as anyone."

The Charlie Cooke Years

1966   Bought for a Chelsea record £72,500 from Dundee.
1967   FA Cup runner-up in Chelsea's first Wembley Cup Final.
1968   Chelsea Player of the Year.
1970   FA Cup winner, Chelsea's first FA Cup triumph.
1971   European Cup Winners' Cup winner, Chelsea's first European triumph.
1972   League Cup runner-up.
1972   Sold to Crystal Palace for £85,000.
1974   Bought from Crystal Palace for £17,000.
1975   Chelsea Player of the Year.
1978   Moved to America to be player-coach at Memphis Rogues having played 373 games and scored 30 goals.

The big, blond, goal-den boy

Kerry
Dixon

Kerry Dixon was the last of an English breed but the first of a Chelsea era. He was a powerful, pacy, high-jumping, goalscoring, blond No. 9 hero.

Rejected by Tottenham Hotspur at eighteen after top-scoring in their youth team, he dropped into non-League football with Dunstable, then worked his way up: 1983, old Third Division Golden Boot winner with Reading; 1984, old Second Division Golden Boot winner with Chelsea; 1985, top flight Golden Boot winner with Chelsea. He also won his first England cap, and scored twice on his first England start that year. It would be almost impossible to take that road now.

Increasingly in the 1980s, as more money came into football, a player's career was improved by moving clubs on a regular basis. For Kerry Dixon, however, once he had settled at Chelsea there was to be no other club in his heart. He was determined to stay as long as possible. His heart went against his wallet and he followed it.

In the end he remained for nine years and scored 193 goals, just nine fewer than the Chelsea record of 202 hit by Bobby Tambling. When, two years after leaving, he found himself in an FA Cup semi-final with Luton Town at Wembley against Chelsea, he was treated to a unique experience, the whole ground – fans from both sides – chanting his name before and after the game. It is unlikely that has happened to anyone else.

For Chelsea he was a new era. The club was at its lowest-ever ebb in 1983, having avoided relegation to the old Division Three only in the penultimate game of the season. A win at Bolton Wanderers sent Bolton down. Defeat would have sucked Chelsea down instead.

Dixon arrived that summer and started banging in the goals. Chelsea won the division, and challenged for major trophies immediately.

Critics – and there were many – said that he didn't have a good enough first touch for the very top level. He shrugged off the comments like he shrugged off many a defender as he latched on to a ball over the top of the back line: "I may not have the best first touch, but my last one is pretty good," he hit back.

There are a number of reasons why Kerry Dixon makes the Chelsea Top Ten. There's the sheer number of goals, and his loyalty to the club. There's his relationship with the fans, his time for them at all times, and his general ambassadorial way. Even in bad times he was always a good news story. And there was the way he adapted his game to become a provider as well as a scorer in his later years.

He is different to many other footballers. It is not a secret that he has lost a fortune with his gambling. But that is how he is. He's not a person to go through life regretting anything. He knows how to enjoy himself. He likes a good time. Perhaps he was the last generation of players who were able to spend a whole career having a good time. That didn't make him unprofessional. But it did help make him close to the fans.

There's one more reason why he has to be in here. He's my mate, and he might not talk to me again if he doesn't make the list. Well, not so much talk as argue! We argue all the time – about football. He loves talking the game. Typically, the interview for this book takes place in a pub.

Supping his lager-top he chuckles at his 'last touch' jibe back at the critics. "I meant it!" he says forcefully. "I admit your first touch is important. Holding the ball up was not a particular strength of mine. Mark Hughes, now he could hold the ball up brilliantly, but he never scored 20 goals in a season. I did it five out of nine." Five seasons out of nine, and over 30 in each of his first two.

"My first touch wasn't the best. But if I got two, with the second touch it was in the net. These days people do demand a good first touch. But Didier Drogba hasn't got the best, and he scored over 30 goals in a season. And rightly, people are happy with that."

Dixon was one of those players who got written off more times than most, and kept bouncing back with more goals. When he talks, he bristles with the determination he possessed throughout his career to keep him going. "I always had an unswerving belief in my ability. No-one likes taking knocks, but when you take one and it's an injustice in your head, you go out to show it's an injustice."

So he stayed and he played and he scored and he scored again, and he suffered the bad times together with the fans – and there were plenty of them – and he led the way to the better times, and the fans loved him for it. Does he think he has been old fashioned?

"You're joking. Look at this clobber! Old fashioned, my arse! Okay, I was never a trend-setter. I'd always wanted to play football, I loved scoring goals, I loved being a winner."

On the evening of Friday 15th September, 1989, he got into a drinking session with some friends, and somehow it didn't stop. He didn't put an end to it until 4.30am on Saturday when he was very happy. At three o'clock that afternoon he was standing in the centre-circle at White Hart Lane, ready to kick off against Tottenham.

He laughs when that story is brought up. "You mean I did it again? Surprisingly! We won 4-1, I scored my 150th League goal and got 10 out of 10 in *The Sun*." He shrugs, as if shrugging off another defender, smiles to himself and sups on his lager-top once more.

Kerry Dixon was a Luton boy. Now he's a Dunstable man. Dunstable is next to Luton. Like Jimmy Greaves; he loves his home environment.

He was picked up by Tottenham as a youngster and worked his way through their ranks, completing his apprenticeship in the youth team. But then he was discarded. Knock number one! "I scored 31 goals, I was top scorer in the South-East Counties League and they let me go. They said they had Terry Gibson, Mark Falco, Colin Lee, Ian Moores and a fellow called Jimmy Bolton.

"They said I lost 3-2 on a vote. Peter Shreeves and Ron Henry voted for me, but Keith Burkinshaw and Billy Nicholson didn't. Shreevesie said afterwards it was one of their biggest mistakes, he said that every time I went back I seemed to score against Tottenham. And I did! It was my favourite ground because I always scored there."

Shreeves, later a very successful assistant-manager to Glenn Hoddle at Chelsea, offered to organise him trials at West Ham and Orient. "I said, no thanks, I'll sort myself out. I'd started at Cheshunt, I'd had a year there, and Brendan McNally who was actually the guy who broke Roy Dwight's leg in the 1959 FA Cup Final, he'd moved to managing Dunstable, so I went there.

"All the managers who got the best out of me, they wanted me. If they didn't want me, no problem! I had a carefree attitude. I couldn't care less. I'd go and play non-League. That's how I am.

"It may have been a defence-mechanism, but internally I'd

say 'I'll show those tw*ts'. And I did! I got 51 goals in the Southern League and was top scorer. I played for England Amateurs against Italy and scored." And he got signed by Reading.

Towards the end of his three years at Reading, the Chelsea management team of John Neal and Ian McNeil went to watch him play at Gillingham. He missed three one-on-ones with the goalkeeper. It didn't put them off. They signed him that summer for £175,000. It was the biggest Chelsea signing of the summer, but well down on the club record of £225,000 which had been set as long ago as 1974, nine years before, for David Hay.

Dixon isn't the slightest bit affected in his assessment of himself by those misses at Gillingham. "I know what happened, they said he got three one-on-ones, he got them when other people didn't get them. If he got them for us, I think he'd score.

"For me, Ian Rush was the one who scored with the most chances. One chance, Rush, 1-0. But most players needed three or four. When I missed a chance for England against Northern Ireland I knew I'd get another chance. That was my attitude. But I didn't because I didn't get selected, and that's what happens at the higher level. If I'd have played more there I'd have adapted. Gary Lineker was in the team and he was paired with Peter Beardsley and got the chances one after another and scored the goals."

He made his Chelsea debut against promotion favourites Derby in the first game of the season at Stamford Bridge. Chelsea won 5-0 and went on to win the division. He scored twice. Those goals were important to him. They were the fourth and fifth. Fellow debutant Nigel Spackman, left-back Chris Hutchings and winger Clive Walker had already netted.

"I'd finished the season before for Reading as top scorer, and they got relegated, and yes I was perturbed at 3-0. The

team was doing well against a side that was fancied, and I
wanted to score. I got the chance, and I got the last couple."

Next game he got one at Gillingham – yes, Gillingham – in a
League Cup first round, first-leg win, then two at Brighton in a
2-1 victory and, although he didn't score in the next two
games, he followed up with all four in the 4-0 second-leg
success against the Gills. Five games and he had arrived.

"It was a great feeling, my first hat-trick for the club. We
were on a roll, and I wanted to score more and more goals,
and I'd got off to a bit of a flyer. We realised we had a pretty
decent side. We gelled very well."

Already the Shed, where the terraced fans collected to give
the most impassioned support, were singing 'There's Only
One Kerry Dixon' across south-west London. With each goal
the big No. 9 launched two powerful big arms in the air and
smiled the Kerry smile.

There were a couple of two-goal performances to come in
October away wins, at Huddersfield Town and Fulham, but all
was not well. His strike partner, Colin Lee, wasn't scoring. And
Lee's old strike partner, David Speedie, was complaining he
wasn't in the team. Lee and Speedie were friends. They didn't
make life comfortable for Kerry.

In the end, John Neal switched to Speedie instead of Lee. In
their first home game together, Dixon and Speedie helped tear
apart Newcastle United, more promotion favourites with
Keegan, Beardsley, Waddle and McDermott in their team.
Speedie scored twice in a 4-0 win. But competitive Speedie
continued to moan even when he was playing – he still is
moaning by the way, but we love him for it now – and when,
after a 1-0 home defeat to Manchester City, another
promotion-possible side, he went for Dixon over missed
opportunities. Dixon chinned him.

Thereafter they formed one of the great strike partnerships
of Chelsea history. Kerry's gone through the story so many

times, and to him it was a necessary difficult birth to a great relationship.

"Speedo kicked up about not being in the side. I was scoring goals and Speedo wasn't happy. The famous spat came around December, the Manchester City game. Off the field there was animosity because of David's relationship with Colin. David had got there six months before me, but once we'd had our spat, got a few things in the open, we let the manager pick the side and our partnership was even better.

"Speedo had kept chivvying away, I'd kept scoring goals, but in this game he kept on that he was setting up chances, so in the end I said I'd see him after the game, and I went in and smacked him. He came back at me and John Neal called us in. He said: 'You're not getting dropped so you'd better learn to play with each other.' So we shook hands, had a little cuddle and found the best partnership of our lives.

"He was a good player. He'd got his opportunity and it worked well. He worked hard, he was tenacious. I continued to play my game, and he was fitting into the parts I wasn't so good at.

"It really was the best partnership of my life. He had a great first touch, he worked so hard...all the things I didn't do! John Neal pulled us in the office one day and said: 'David, you're doing great, but you've got to score more goals.' He got the hump, and you know what? I felt for him! Next game on the Saturday we were away to West Brom and Speedo got two. So it worked.

"Good manager, great partnership."

The Dixon-Speedie partnership became unstoppable. With Pat Nevin introduced on the right-wing, It was a rampant, high-scoring team which won the Second Division Championship for the first time in the club's history. Dixon's pace and aerial ability, Nevin's twists and turns, Speedie's link-up play and pressing all made for a variety of attacking styles within the set-up.

Dixon loved playing for Neal. "His philosophy was simple. Give it to Pat. A lot of people didn't understand. Pat was a creative player. We had John Bumstead, Nigel Spackman, two hard-working, understated midfield players. Pat wanted to beat players and cross when he wanted to cross, chip it up to the far post and I'd come over the top and bang! I'd score! Speedo wanted it played in early, but once he'd learned it, it was the best trio I ever played in. It was special.

"The more we played together, the better it got. You knew when Pat had the ball he'd take someone on, the centre-half would be marking you in the box, and you wouldn't make any movement because you knew when Pat was going to cross it. Pat would probably try to beat the defender again! And knowing that just gave us the edge. The three of us were very good as a unit."

His first League hat-trick for Chelsea was in the home 5-0 win over Leeds United which earned promotion. He still loves the day. "All of the days you think you'd never forget are probably down to the supporters. The Leeds fans were kicking up a bit on the far side, the Chelsea fans were coming on the pitch near the end. Paul Canoville, I think, scored the fifth goal, the fans were just coming, they'd already been on at 4-0 and the ref blew up and they thought it was all over. They were going to be allowed on at the end. But I'd scored a hat-trick, and I've got to be honest, I was thinking, 'heh, I hope we get them off because I can see this game being abandoned.' There were a few minutes left to play.

"But the referee said, 'as soon as we kick-off get yourselves on the touchline and I'll blow up', and that's exactly what we did. The fans came on, there was a sea of Chelsea supporters and it really was a great day."

Two weeks later he scored the goal at Grimsby Town which

won the title. "Again, the sea of supporters coming back down the motorway afterwards, the sea of blue all around the ground, all over, spilling over the top...I think the game got delayed because of the number of fans trying to get into the small ground. It was a fantastic day."

It was a typical goal. Nevin cross, Dixon header.

In all competitions he got 34 goals that season, and won the divisional Golden Boot with 28. But his next goal, the first of the following season, his first in the top flight, the old Division One, was to be his most precious. For him, it was the moment he really proved that Tottenham had made a mistake in getting rid of him.

The match was at Highbury. It finished 1-1. "The goal didn't mean I'd arrived, but it meant I could cut it if I had the chance. And the Chelsea fans at the Clock End will always live with me. The fans again! And to draw at Arsenal, a team full of internationals, one of the more favoured sides in the division, meant we could cut it."

It was a good goal, Dixon driving a Speedie flick and finding his effort well saved by Pat Jennings, but responding with high technique to the rebound to belt it into the net. Up went the arms, up went the jump, up went the 6,000 Chelsea fans standing behind the goal. Dixon cherishes the photograph of the celebration.

But that climax was followed by a trough, a knock. Having hit his goal-den goal he hit a brick wall, a dry run. He couldn't score again.

"Seven games, I think it was. It did concern me. Every time I didn't score in a game it did concern me. I wanted to score goals. And when goalscorers aren't getting goals, people often say they're not contributing, which was one of the accusations levelled at me. I can understand that. But I started again after seven games and went on to be top scorer in the division."

There were two goals against Millwall in the League Cup,

two each against Leicester, Watford and Ipswich, and then his first top-flight hat-trick. Coventry had taken a two-goal lead at Stamford Bridge. Chelsea won 6-2.

"It was a muddy old day, Kilcline and Trevor Peake were the centre-halves, we were all over them and I got three. My first First Division matchball meant a lot. Firsts were always special, my first England goal, my first hat-trick."

Everyone was talking about Dixon and Speedie, and in particular Kerry Dixon. He was still only 23-years-old, and he was producing the goods on a home pitch which, despite the openness of the stadium, was mostly a bog. He smiles at the thought of the technical requirements needed to shine on that.

"Technology has moved forward and you rarely get bobbles now. I never had the luck to play against Barcelona and deal with those factors. But I had to deal with the pitch. Peter Osgood was the same before me. Now people don't have those situations. If it was played on the floor and you wanted to score, you always had to take into account the possible bobble. The game has changed. We always knew, if a player looked good when the ball rolled well in September, we needed to ask what would they be like in winter at Wigan?"

This was such an exciting time for Chelsea fans. After five years in the old Second Division, here were heroes developed at Stamford Bridge – not youth products but low-priced bargain buys – taking the country by storm and challenging for European qualification with uninhibited attacking football.

He scored one of his best goals against European champions Liverpool. "I took it off Hansen on their left side, cut inside, kept looking to cross for someone, went past Lawrenson, and in the end I found myself virtually level with the near post, and made to cross and slipped it inside Grobbelaar with my left foot." The nation started calling for him to play for England.

Goals were coming in every competition. He'd struck a League Cup hat-trick against Manchester City in November, and in January he achieved that midweek hat-trick – in fact four goals – at Wigan in an FA Cup third-round replay.

Come the end of the season, Chelsea finished sixth and he achieved sharing the Golden Boot with Gary Lineker having scored 24 League goals. In all competitions he notched 36.

"The Golden Boot was important for me," he admits without qualms. "Myself, Gary Lineker, there were quite a few strikers around getting goals, Mariner and Woodcock got a few at Arsenal, the battle was really on and it developed into a head-to-head at the end with Gary, and in the end we shared it. It was a relief. After the battle we had we both got the accolade and we both deserved it."

And that summer, England beckoned. He was called up by manager Bobby Robson for a tournament in Mexico, one year before the World Cup there. In his first start he scored twice against West Germany, one an uncertain prod, one a thunderous header. He notched two more in his next game against the United States.

Kerry Dixon, Chelsea legend, had arrived.

Chelsea's attacking may have been uninhibited in outlook, but it was limited in practice. Throughout his nine years, Kerry Dixon was served ammunition by a succession of wingers: Walker, Nevin, Canoville, Thomas, McAllister, Wise, Stuart, Le Saux...but in midfield he was backed up by hard working, honest, responsible players rather than creative ones: Bumstead, Spackman, McAndrew, Nicholas, Dickens, Townsend, Jones.

He scored from crosses, from balls over the top, he scored counter-attacking goals, and he scored in tandem with his partners: Speedie in the early years, and later Gordon Durie or Kevin Wilson.

But in all his time at the club, he only really had one gifted 'No. 10'-style player to create for him through the middle. "Micky Hazard made a lot of goals for me. He was never really a first choice in all his time at the club, but I loved it when he played. It was no good telling several of our players that if I got level with the centre-half, drop it in behind and I'll score, because they couldn't. Micky could."

Who knows how many goals he would have scored if he could have had a Hudson or a Wilkins, a latter-day Wise or a Di Matteo?

His Chelsea career started in the same vein at full-back, the club having defensively-minded ones: Hollins, Jones, Lee, Rougvie, Wood, Dublin. But at least in later years Clarke and Dorigo provided more options.

His firepower was clear. Height, pace. "I don't think anyone could beat me on the sprints. Clive Walker early on, Tony Dorigo, they would say they'd get close, they were the only two, but realistically I was the quickest for the majority of time I was here. Jason Cundy and Frank Sinclair, a couple of youngsters came through later on. There was always a good battle in the sprints."

Whenever things seemed unable to get any better, another knock was lurking for Kerry Dixon. The good life just wouldn't expand to one hundred per cent of all activity.

In his third season, the goals were flooding in again, and Chelsea were real title contenders. By the turn of the year he had scored 21 goals, 12 in the League. There were two strike partnerships feared most in the country, Dixon-Speedie at Chelsea and Dalglish-Rush at Liverpool. Which was better? The answer was a constant source of national debate.

When Chelsea drew Liverpool at home in the fourth round of the FA Cup, the nation had a chance to compare the two. Before kick-off, the two top scorers, Dixon and Rush, shook hands and posed for the cameras. There was utmost respect for each other.

But when the game began it turned into a disaster for Chelsea, and especially for Dixon. He collapsed chasing a ball with a stomach injury, and didn't move. After careful treatment he was carried off. He was out for only a month, but when he returned he was a shadow of the legend for a lengthy period.

He acknowledges the difficulties but minimises them. "The injury definitely had its effect. I tore my stomach muscle and when I got back to full fitness is debatable. The pain was still there. I was managing to play, I was managing to run and I went to the World Cup and the heat helped. But every time there was a twinge there was discomfort.

"People say it cost me, people say I lost a yard of pace. But at the '86 World Cup over thirty yards I was still the fastest for England. I'd be with Gary Lineker going over the line. And there was Kenny Sansom, Gary Stevens of Everton, Viv Anderson.

"Paul McGrath said in his testimonial programme that I was the greatest player he ever played against. That's high praise indeed from a World Cup centre-half who played against great strikers. But if it wasn't Tottenham I was scoring against, it was Manchester United. I always used to score against them as well. I scored two at Old Trafford when I came back that sealed my World Cup place, proved my fitness.

"I used to score against Everton a lot when they were top dogs, and Liverpool with Hansen and Lawrenson. But after that injury, it took a while to get back. How long? I don't know. I'd had two very good years before the injury, and I had two very good years after in 1988-90."

His injury wasn't the only problem in 1985-86. Despite Chelsea going for the title, there was unrest with the new manager. John Hollins, a real Chelsea legend as a player, had succeeded John Neal, and the manager and his centre-forward didn't see eye to eye.

"It was his first job and he didn't fancy me. He dropped me for the last game as I was going to the World Cup and played Gordon Durie. It didn't work, but if it had I'm pretty sure he would have finished up with Gordon Durie and Speedo up front.

"It goes back to what I was saying. If people don't want me, I can't care less. I just don't want to be involved. It picked up under Bobby Campbell, he wanted me to play and I delivered. We survived the first season after John Neal on his euphoria, and then it went downhill."

Even in the heights of 1984-85, the knocks had started: defeat in the League Cup semi-final to relegation-bound Sunderland; and then defeat at home to Norwich City in the last League game which meant no UEFA Cup qualification (the Heysel disaster followed that summer and as a result no English teams competed the next season anyway).

Now, as a result of the stomach injury and the Hollins effect, Dixon's own performances tailed off. He scored just those goals at Manchester United in the remainder of the season to finish with 14 in the League, 23 overall. And then he followed with two dismal years, scoring 26 in total, losing Speedie who was sold to Coventry, not always being the first choice, and in the end Chelsea became the only team to be relegated from the top flight in a play-off.

There was massive unrest in the playing squad, at one time ten players had asked for a transfer, and Dixon seemed certain to go when Hollins agreed a move with two clubs. Dixon even said his goodbyes after one game in the dressing room. But his heart was never in moving, and neither was his chairman's heart in allowing him to move.

"Ken Bates played a major part in me not leaving," he admits. "John Hollins had agreed while Ken was on one of his trips up the Amazon somewhere that I could talk to West Ham and Arsenal. He was prepared to let me go, he had done a deal with both clubs.

"So I spoke to both clubs, and I said 'okay, I'll give you an answer when the chairman gets back.' He came back and told me not to go to training but to go to his house. He asked me what was going on – what he knew and what he didn't know I don't know, but he was chairman of the club and I'm pretty sure he must have known a degree of it – and he said the bottom line was he didn't want me to go. I had two years left on the contract, he said: 'What I'm going to do is offer you another two years!'

"So I said if the deal's okay by me I'll sign. So we thrashed out a new deal, I signed and John Hollins got the sack a week later!"

If Kerry Dixon had gone then, with nearly three great goalscoring years and just over two unhappy, unsuccessful ones in his locker, he would have been a top Chelsea player, but not a Top Ten one. That was about to change.

Defeat to Sunderland, defeat to Norwich, savage League defeats over Easter 1986 (4-0 at home to West Ham, 6-0 at QPR) breaking the title dream, missing a Wembley victory in the Full Members Cup Final over Manchester City, relegation: Kerry took the knocks as badly as the fans.

"Norwich, it was a dreadful pitch and we never should have played. It was all puddles, the ball didn't run true. We should have qualified for Europe. Any time else we would have won the game.

"Sunderland, when Speedo and Clive Walker had a famous incident – there were loads of near misses. The Members Cup was tough. I took it on the chin. I couldn't play, I had a fitness test but I couldn't play. It mattered. I wanted to score goals, I wanted to play games. It hurt. On the day Colin Lee and David Speedie scored five between them. It was brilliant for them.

"The play-offs were a joke. We were the only team ever to get relegated finishing fourth from bottom. Our experience made people think it was unfair. It was stopped after that."

For the record on the 'famous incident', Chelsea had allowed Walker to leave and he was sold to Sunderland. He scored two and made one as they won the semi-final, second leg of the League Cup at Stamford Bridge, and he asked Speedie towards the end of the game if he wanted any tickets for the final. Speedie threw a punch, was sent off, and later in the Players' Bar attacked him, and the two had to be separated by the giant Micky Droy. David Speedie was a top Chelsea player, but he would be a Top Ten Chelsea fighter!

Back to square one, now partnered either with Gordon Durie when fit, or Kevin Wilson, and often with both with one playing wide, Kerry Dixon had something to prove. He did it. In the second Second Division championship year he scored 28 goals, 25 in the League; and in the next season back in the top flight he scored 25, 20 in the League.

"We came back comfortably. It was a bit of an anti-climax because we were a very good side. We played pretty much as a three-pronged attack. Gordon Durie was strong and pacy, Kevin Wilson was technically good, and all three of us did pretty well.

"The first year back up we came fifth, the highest Chelsea had been in twenty years. It felt like a new lease of life. It was a fairytale first time around, but the second time with a new team I knew I could play. I always had confidence in myself at the highest level to score goals. It was a very strong side. We were capable of challenging at the top of the League.

"It's a shame. If it had been the Chelsea of now, we could have made a couple of signings and gone on and won it then."

His new manager was Bobby Campbell. "I knew I was better than what I'd been showing. In a way, goalscorers are 'confidence' players. They need to be believed in. I wasn't getting that from John Hollins and he's entitled to his opinion."

He hadn't scored a hat-trick since December 1985, but in the Second Division he knocked four past Barnsley at home including one outstanding long-distance strike, and the following season he got the perfect hat-trick in the last game at Millwall. "I think Graeme Le Saux created the first, a great ball far post, a header; then it was an excellent curling, right-foot shot; and the third I went on a little bit of a mazy (run), something I'm not associated with, and I finished up putting it in with my left."

That season he was also a trophy winner at Wembley, the renamed Full Members Cup was now the Zenith Data Systems Cup. Tony Dorigo got the only goal of the game against Middlesbrough. "It was a great occasion, we filled the stadium. It was a trophy Ken Bates had created from his time on the FA. I didn't play great but Chelsea won the game. Football players don't play well every week, but for me good players don't have many bad games. Your standard of performance stays high."

Calls for him to be restored in the England squad for the 1990 World Cup were ignored by Bobby Robson, but he was truly unlucky not to be selected. By now he was a better all-round player than the England player of 1985 and '86, even if he may not have been quite as fast.

"There's a little tinge of regret, I wish Bobby Robson who picked me as an England international had picked me a little bit more when I was playing well. There was quite a battle going on, Mark Hateley, Trevor Francis, Tony Cottee, Woodcock, Mariner, there were lots of players in and around the set-up, Gary Lineker of course and Peter Beardsley, and that partnership in effect ended my chances to be an England striker on a regular basis."

He had another two years in the Chelsea side, but never

rekindled the pace or drive to the same degree. Yet he continued to develop as a player, and became someone who would use the wings a lot more and revealed a magnificent crossing style in his make-up.

"That team was a side which was more than confident playing the ball around, and it was a side that could battle. All the years of people badgering me, saying you've got to do more for the team, had finally taken its toll. I'd gathered the experience, I'd still managed to keep the goalscoring desires, and I was creating a lot more chances for the likes of Kevin Wilson and Gordon Durie."

In his final season he scored only six goals. The legs weren't the same. There had been more heartache: another semi-final League Cup defeat, now to Second Division Sheffield Wednesday; an FA Cup replay quarter-final defeat to Second Division Sunderland (yes, them again!).

His final goal, away to Norwich City, was one of his best. "It was a great goal," he smiles with pride. "I loved that one. I didn't know it was my last goal, but I had this feeling it might be. Clarkey (Steve Clarke) played the ball in, I turned, left-foot from the edge of the area, 1-0 away!"

He was on his fourth manager now, Ian Porterfield, and with just nine goals to go to equal Bobby Tambling's record 202 strikes for Chelsea, he was sold to Southampton.

"I loved it, I wouldn't change anything. The fans were unconditionally great to me. From being a Luton supporter as a kid, starting on the terraces, now I'm a Chelsea supporter as they gave me the best nine years of my footballing life.

"Not getting the record is the biggest regret of my footballing life. But it happens. Look at Gary Lineker, one off the England record. I'm proud of my achievements, I'm proud of scoring the goals I scored for Chelsea. I really loved every moment of it.

"The most important thing is I'm the second highest scorer in Chelsea history. The most gutting thing is I should have got 203. I wish it could have been different. But then I wouldn't have had the Luton experience, I wouldn't have had the semi-final.

"And Bobby Tambling, by the way, is a great man. He said he was waiting for the day his record went to me. He's a lovely man. The more people who are prepared to say you're a nice bloke is the most important thing, and Bobby's a really nice bloke. I'd rather be on 193 and second than on 210 and an a***-hole!"

And Kerry is, above all, a lovely bloke. In his prime, in his rise, in his fall, he was always the last player to leave the ground, talking to staff, talking to other players, talking to journalists, talking to fans, and of course enjoying the odd drink.

He is adamant that he was doing the right thing. "There's nothing wrong with a bit of manners in life. People in any walk of life, the Press have jobs to do, the fans, people want to talk to people. And if they take a little time, what's wrong with spending an extra 20 minutes here and there with people?

"I didn't do it to make the Press happy, or even just to make the fans happy, it was that they're stood out in the cold waiting to talk to you, you can at least show a bit of respect back."

But with all that fulfilment, there was so much heartache. "Sunderland the second time round, they got the winner two minutes from time when Andy Townsend lost his marker and Gordon Armstrong scored a goal. Sheffield Wednesday, we never performed. Mentally we weren't right. Something was missing. On any day we had a better team than them. But if the best team wins every week, you could pick the League ahead of the season.

"We had two good teams and should have won something.

Obviously we lacked something. We had two good sides and were beaten by teams we never should have been beaten by. We lost silly games. We weren't good enough mentally."

That should be the end of the story. Kerry Dixon was the fans' special hero for nine years. Now he had gone. But on Saturday 9th April, 1994, almost two years after his sad exit, Chelsea finally reached an FA Cup semi-final for the first time since 1970, and Kerry's Luton joined them there. The match was staged at Wembley. He was 32-years-old.

It was such an emotional occasion for Chelsea fans. It was the first season under the management of Glenn Hoddle. When the teams walked on to the pitch, the Chelsea fans spine-chillingly sang 'Chelsea Are Back'. But then, rather than sing the names of their own players, the song that thundered around the old stadium was 'One Kerry Dixon'. The old legend was back as well. He was embarrassed as he gave his traditional thumbs up to the opposition crowd.

Chelsea won 2-0. As he trudged off, a semi-final loser again, the Chelsea fans erupted even louder. "One Kerry Dixon, there's only one Kerry Dixon..." He had to walk almost the length of the pitch to the tunnel with his song ringing in his ears.

"Without a doubt it was the most humbling moment of my entire career. Chelsea fans made it special for me. Luton fans often say to me they found it really strange, they were trying to cheer their team, and they couldn't even cheer their team off for the Cup run they'd had, being the underdogs, because of the noise from the fans who were singing about me.

"I'd lost a semi-final, yet the great Chelsea fans made it special for me rather than just celebrating going to their first FA Cup Final for 24 years. That undoubtedly was the best moment of my career."

For Kerry Dixon, man of the people, it was the people who

cheered every one of his 193 goals which made him special.

These days Kerry is still active at the club of his heart. He is a regular on *Chelsea TV*; a matchday host for the corporate supporters; the co-commentator on all home games and many away for *Smooth FM* radio; the most in-demand presenter of the Legend's Tour around Stamford Bridge; in-demand as a pundit by *Sky Sports* and he also does a lot of personal appearances at various events. He is still living for today, he loves a good goalscorer – he loved Jimmy Floyd Hasselbaink – and he loves talking to people who follow the club. Chelsea's second-highest goalscorer has achieved that rare status of modern legends, he is one of the people.

Kerry Dixon on his favourite Chelsea goal

"It would be the one at Arsenal, the first in the First Division, because of the sight of all the Chelsea fans at the Clock End, and what it meant to me and what it meant to the club."

Pat Nevin on his favourite Kerry Dixon goal

"I think the Grimsby Town goal away from home. We won the League with that goal. It was a wee classic of what we'd done a few times. I went down the line, I knew exactly where he'd be and laid it up for him. He still had a lot to do because he had to come over a few defenders. It made me look good because few centre-forwards would have got it. It not only won us the League but it got me out of jail because I'd missed a penalty!"

David Speedie on his favourite Kerry Dixon goal

"He scored that many! The most important was against Grimsby when we won the title. The hat-trick against Leeds got us promoted. The header at Manchester City towards the end of the season, near post, when I crossed it! Sometimes you thought he was crossing it and it flew into the top corner. He didn't score spectacular goals though, headers and tap-ins from me and Pat!!! So I definitely can't give you one goal, there were just so, so many!"

Kevin Wilson on his favourite Kerry Dixon goal

"We played Millwall the year we came fifth. It was the best hat-trick I've seen, a left foot, a right foot and a header. So there's three of my favourites! And they were all quality finishes. One was from the edge of the area. You won't see people score goals like he did. He'll always live in Chelsea's history."

Steve Clarke on his favourite Kerry Dixon goal

"There were a lot of strong headers and a lot of balls in behind when his pace and his power took him through. He didn't place them so much, he liked to belt them. He wasn't one to get a back-flick, a Zola-type of goal, he just used his qualities and kept churning them out. I remember a game against Barnsley when he got four, and I think there was another right-foot, left-foot, header in there."

Chelsea's All-Time Top Scorers

Bobby Tambling	202
Kerry Dixon	193
Roy Bentley	150
Peter Osgood	150
Jimmy Greaves	132

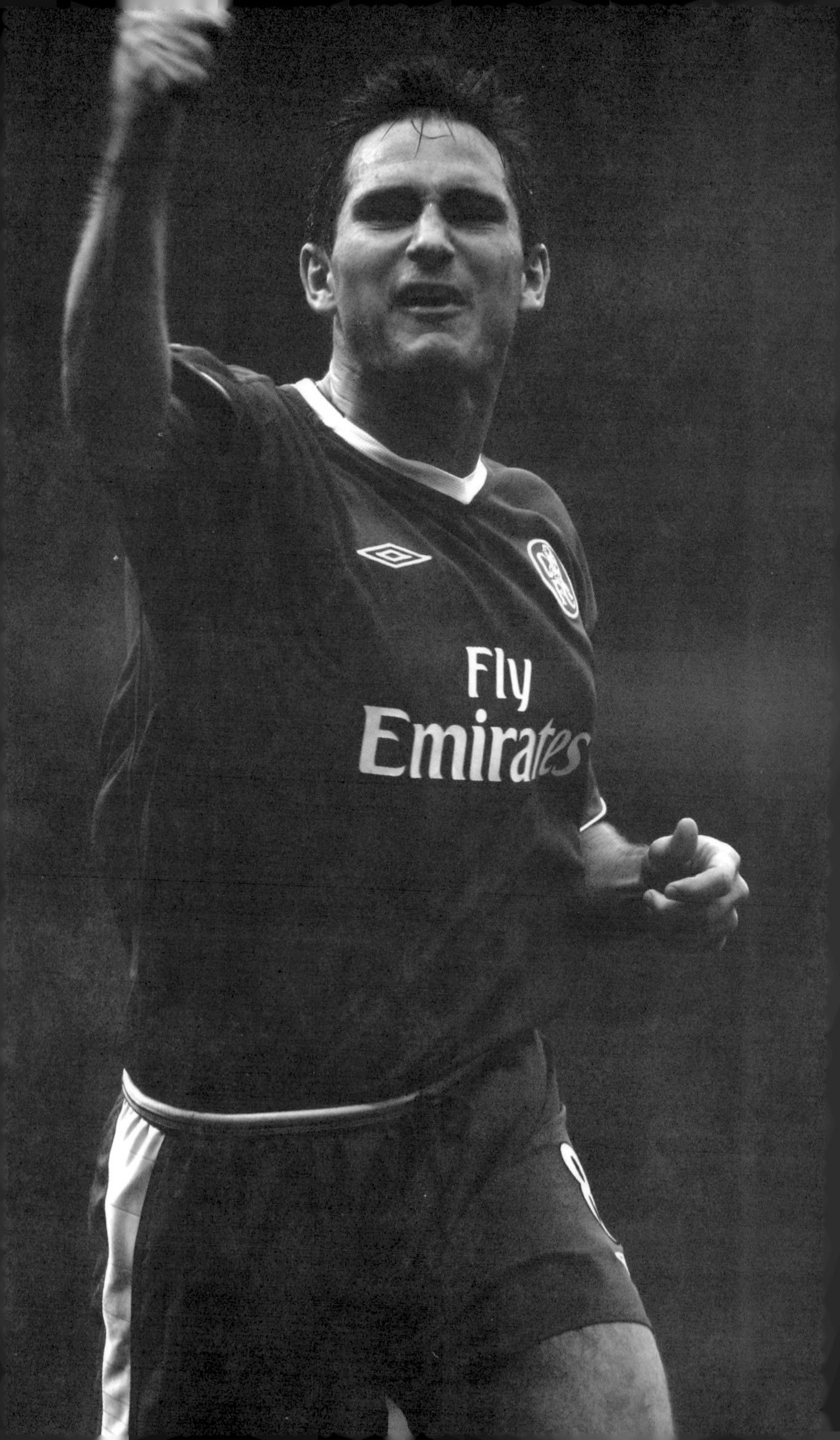
Fly
Emirates

Moving on a level...and on, and on, and on

Frank
Lampard

"Big fat, big fat Frank; big fat, big fat Frank..." sing the West Ham fans year after year to the midfielder they sold to Chelsea. It is the same tune as Chelsea fans use for him. "Super, super Frank; super, super Frank..."

Frank Lampard, son of the West Ham coach, nephew of their manager, made his debut at seventeen, played for England, but was booed by the home fans on more than one occasion. He was booed by them regularly. When Frank Lampard senior was sacked with brother-in-law Harry Redknapp, Frank junior wanted a move straight away. West Ham got a whopping £11m from Chelsea.

"... Big fat, big fat Frank..." West Ham were relegated two seasons later.

However, the world thought Chelsea mad to pay so much for Lampard. Only Jimmy Floyd Hasselbaink, a top goalscorer, had cost the club more at that point. At Chelsea Lampard had a moderate first season, a good second one, a blinding third and a sensational fourth. At the end of that year he was voted the second best player in the world by FIFA.

But still the West Ham fans sang. "... Big fat Frankie Lampard!"

He shook his head in private after another Chelsea win over his former team in late 2007. He had been at Chelsea for six years and for three of them had been considered one of the best midfielders on the planet. Still the West Ham fans sang. He had taken to pulling his shorts tight round his thighs to show off his perfect muscular finish. Now, in off-duty clothes, he smiled conspiratorially and whispered: "The only thing that's fat about me now is my wallet!"

I laughed and my eyes danced with anticipation. "And, no, you can't use that!" he emphasised before I could ask. He could imagine how it would be misinterpreted. But, sorry Frank, it's too good a line to dismiss. And it's what those West Ham fans deserve. Anyway, if any of them are reading this, they'll be sympathising with you.

Colin Hutchinson, Chelsea's managing director through the 1990s and up to 2002, had decided to splash the cash on Lampard in 2001. It was a time of regeneration. When he announced how much the player was costing at the press conference to introduce him, there was real disbelief. Hutchinson added that as a midfield goalscorer he would be replacing the recently sold and much-loved Gustavo Poyet. That was a big challenge both football-wise and emotionally.

It was also slightly disingenuous. Poyet played from wide, mostly on the left. Lampard played through the middle. Goal-wise he might have been destined to replace Poyet, but positionally he was replacing the even more legendary, loved and valued Dennis Wise, also sold in the summer. It seemed an impossible task.

Now retired, living in Eastbourne, Hutchinson chuckles down the phone. His voice is as gravel-based as ever on its one-time smoker foundation. "Eleven million pounds!" he states, almost as a joke. "Everyone says he was an absolute snip now."

He's right. Frank was an absolute snip.

Something went right with Lampard straight away. Before his debut, I introduced him to the crowd on the pitch along with all the other new summer signings. One by one I went through them, leaving him until last because he was the biggest investment. His name received the loudest welcome. He was cheered. He had been concerned at how he would be received in West London after a career in East London, and he was welcomed like he had come to his new home.

But he had been a West Ham player. He had won nothing. The previous season West Ham had finished fifteenth. Wise and Poyet had won European trophies, FA Cups, League Cups, they had challenged for the Premier League title. Lampard's only medal was for the South-East Counties League Cup, ironically won at Stamford Bridge against Chelsea. Chelsea had won 4-1 at Upton Park in the first leg of the youth team final. West Ham, inspired by a schoolboy attacking midfielder by the name of Rio Ferdinand, won 5-2 in the second leg. The game went to penalties. Lampard scored the winning penalty. He liked big tasks then. He was up to the massive one now.

You will not find anywhere in football anyone with the same self-willed determination, the same blind self-belief to be not just good enough for the task, but to be the best. The reason Lampard had a moderate first season was because, it appeared to almost everyone, he was a moderate player. He admits his mental streak is unique.

"I've been strong-willed from the beginning," he says with strange detachment rather than pride. He's a pretty regular bloke when he's not being a world-class footballer. He is sitting with a cappuccino and a bottle of water and chatting. "I've had, not setbacks, but things I've had to achieve. I've had to prove people wrong. I had to get into the West Ham team, I had to get to Chelsea and play. I enjoy having a focus, a challenge. Countless times I could see when people doubted me, and I went on to do it, at West Ham, at Chelsea and with England.

"It gets easier, actually. You go on to have more belief. I've more belief now than as an 18-year-old."

But what gave him this massive drive to improve, and not just improve by degrees but from moderate to the best in the world? "An element was born into me, I guess, and an element of it was pushed in me by my dad. He's a very strong character, possibly stronger than me. He made sure I wouldn't accept failure, and I am scared of it. I wanted to be perfect. I know I never will be, but I'll get as close as possible."

Chelsea drew on Lampard's debut. It was a new midfield. Jesper Grønkjær had been signed the previous December, but Emmanuel Petit in the centre next to Lampard and Boudewijn Zenden on the left made their debuts too. Zenden gave Chelsea an early lead, then Newcastle scored a late equaliser.

The new Chelsea was disappointing. They finished sixth, as they had the season before, and only qualified for the UEFA Cup through being FA Cup runners-up to double-winning Arsenal. It wasn't a disaster, particularly for Lampard. He had never finished so high with West Ham and had never been anywhere near a Cup Final.

The problem was, he didn't do anything match winning. "I know what you're going to say," he laughs. "John Bumstead!" This is true. John Bumstead was a great Chelsea servant who played 409 games and was a dogged midfielder. He was the kind of person who was one of the first names on the team sheet. But he wasn't an £11m player. In his day that would have been Kerry Dixon, the match winner.

Lampard, like Bumstead, rarely gave the ball away. But, unlike Wise and Poyet, he rarely made the difference.

"It was a moderate start," he confirms. "But it improved as the season went on culminating in the Cup Final where I had a good game." He'd played his best game up until then in the semi-final win over Fulham, but that final was a revelation. If Marcel Desailly was Chelsea's best player with a performance of unbelievable dominance from centre-back, then it didn't hide Lampard's surprising dominance of Arsenal's midfield powerhouse Patrick Vieira.

Lampard had found challenges to overcome on his way to this performance, doubts to wipe away. "Don't forget I'd played left and right midfield soon after the first game, and that threw me early on. I've got a lot of respect for Ranieri (Chelsea manager Claudio Ranieri) and we got some good results with me there. We won 3-0 at Manchester United, but I came off the pitch feeling I wasn't giving enough. I wasn't contented to be a good cog in the team. It made me push to get my place in the middle."

That season he got just seven goals and six assists. Two years before, when Chelsea had won the FA Cup and reached the quarter-finals of the Champions League, Poyet had scored eighteen goals and Wise ten. Wise had got eleven assists and Poyet seven.

But he didn't falter. He came back for his second season and immediately showed that he had added to his game. No-one has improved year on year like Lampard did at the outset of his Chelsea career. In the first match he scored a late winner as Chelsea came from two down to beat Charlton Athletic 3-2 away. Ten days later he scored the equaliser at Southampton, having started the move to earn a draw. He was affecting games. Before the end of September Chelsea drew 0-0 away to Fulham, the match played at their temporary home of Loftus Road, and suddenly he was offering driving runs through the middle and long-range passing. He was man of the match.

"I remember that game!" he says immediately when it's pulled out as an example. Remembering a 0-0 draw! Obviously he sensed the improvement too.

"It was a very good season," he says with great seriousness, as if he knew how important it had been to step up. "It wasn't an underrated one, but in terms of doing more it was good. I was feeling quicker, I was running with the ball, I felt unafraid of hitting forty-yard balls. I felt a member of the team. I felt I was beginning to drive the team. The fans started to sing my name quite a lot, and I reacted to that. I felt this was my team. I've got great memories of that season. That was me arriving at Chelsea."

There were many memorable moments. Given the long rivalry with Leeds, a 3-2 home win was one of them. Leeds led twice. "I was given one goal but I think I scored two. The Dubious Goals Committee said (Dominic) Matteo put it in. Eidur (Gudjohnsen) scored an incredible goal from my cross for the first." At the time it appeared to be Lampard's first brace for the team. "I was influencing games," he announces with relish.

In the FA Cup at Arsenal he scored a late equaliser to force a replay. "I didn't play particularly well and I got lucky with the late goal. But games when you make a difference with 6,000 travelling fans are important. JT scored too, and me and him were becoming synonymous with Chelsea."

The last game of the season, it turned out, changed his life. Chelsea was broke. The team lay fourth going into the match and needed to draw with fifth-placed Liverpool to qualify for the Champions League and stave off financial breakdown. New chief executive Trevor Birch told the team beforehand how vital it was to earn Champions League money.

"That was a great game to be involved in," Frank recalls now. "Even considering what's happened after that, that game is up there. Trevor Birch told my agent afterwards that he was looking to get me off the wage list if we didn't win. I was a pretty decent earner, and they were facing administration or whatever. If we hadn't won, then my history with Chelsea might have been different."

It still wasn't great. He scored eight goals and managed five assists that season. But so many of the incidents which made up his statistics were crucial this time. The fans voted him Player of the Year runner-up, another important milestone for him. "And if it wasn't for Franco being incredible at the age of thirty-seven or whatever he was, I think I would have won it that year!"

He still hadn't won anything. But he'd played in a Cup Final and now he was going to play in the Champions League. And when he came back for the next season, he was going to play for Roman Abramovich, the club's new owner.

One pre-season Chelsea got in a top heart consultant, and by chance a Chelsea season-ticket holder, to check the players' hearts. Duncan Dymond announced with great joy that Lampard had just about the biggest heart he had ever seen. "An elephant heart!"

Frank wasn't so heartened to hear the news as Dymond was to give it. "When he first told me, I was scared, scared at not having a normal heart. But he told me it was capable of pumping oxygen round my body better than a more normal heart. I like to think I'm one of the fittest players in football, and I do need to work hard. He said I needed to work hard just to get fit, because the heart demands to be worked hard. And I am obsessed with training!"

That's Frank Lampard. Training, eating well in restaurants, watching television (especially *Chelsea TV*, spending time with his parents, and not living the glitzy lifestyle that tabloid newspapers like to depict. He was well prepared for the Abramovich years.

"I moved on a level. I started the season very well. The biggest thing I did was react to the challenge of the new owner. That summer was horrible for me. Having done well the year before I spent the summer reading we had signed this midfielder and that midfielder, so I had to become a bigger person and step up a level again. But I had good games in the Champions League and that was me moving on a level."

Zola and Le Saux had gone. Now there was only Desailly from the 1990s. The new stalwarts were Terry, Lampard, Cudicini, Hasselbaink and Gudjohnsen. But there were so many players who could play central midfield: Makelele, Petit, Gérémi, Verón, Cole…and Lampard.

In his first two seasons he had played more games than anyone else. He had missed nothing through injury. After an early suspension he hadn't missed or not been selected for a League game. The challenge to continue in that vein couldn't have been greater.

In just the second match, the first League game following a Champions League qualifier, he responded. It was at Anfield. With the scores level and three minutes remaining his sublime chip put Jimmy Floyd Hasselbaink in for the winner. Yet again, here was the new Lampard. There had been no defence splitting passes before now.

"It was always there. I just didn't have the confidence to bring it out. Once you feel comfortable in a team, and having the pressure to do it, and being helped by having better people around you, it's easier. In a mediocre team you can get away with being average."

But when Chelsea played the first Champions League Group game, away to Sparta Prague, he was faced with the biggest slap of his career. He was left out. "Me, JT and Eidur sitting on the bench with the absolute hump!" He spits with the pain of that failure, still a strong taste in his mouth. "The things we were saying! Having fought to get us in the Champions League, you can picture how we felt having been shunted on the bench for the new signings.

"Each one of us reacted very well. I think Ranieri made a mistake that night. That's not a dig. He didn't see me, John and Eidur as the bigger part of what was to come. I was a bit selfish that night. I didn't mind us not doing so well in the first half, so I could make the difference."

He did. He came on at half-time for Adrian Mutu and transformed the game. It was the night that Ranieri learned he couldn't play without Frank Lampard; without galloping, probing, motoring Frank Lampard. He didn't make that mistake again.

But there were more improvements to come. Chelsea won 1-0 in Prague, returned to England and won 5-0 at Wolves. Lampard opened the scoring with a scorching 25-yard left-footer. After two years it was his first real, long distance, trademark Lampard goal. Game after game he was adding to his ammunition.

"It was a very good strike with the left foot. It was a time when I was buzzing. I played with Maka (Claude Makelele) that year in a four-man midfield, him and me in central midfield, and we just ran it. Maka helped me a lot. He's one of the best midfielders I've played with. He brought class, discipline and a winning way from Real Madrid. He was so unselfish, a team player, an absolute ideal foil for an attacking midfielder."

The good times gathered pace. At home to Lazio he scored his first Champions League goal, and it was another trademark Lampard drive from distance. "That was another big game mentally for me. I hit the bar with a left-footer from twenty yards and then hit the equaliser. That was me away enjoying Champions League nights, feeling I deserved to be there. Then we won 4-0 away in Rome. I'm quite a humble person deep down, and so that was such a great feeling."

In November the new Chelsea went top of the League with a 1-0 home win over Manchester United. Lampard hit the winning penalty. "I was quite pleased with achieving that. I had to battle to claim the ball. Mutu and Crespo were sniffing, but I grew into that responsibility. I was feeling very confident. I'd scored a penalty the previous week. I was enjoying my football."

Chelsea finished second that season, and reached the semi-final of the Champions League by knocking out Arsenal in the quarters. It was Chelsea's first win over the Gunners since he had joined. He scored the equaliser at Highbury as Chelsea won 2-1, after a home 1-1 draw. In the semi-final he scored a cracking goal at home to Monaco. "That was a great goal. Eidur was involved as I burst through. It's a night I regret. We should have gone to the final. It was one of the first really bad nights as a Chelsea player. But you're going to have them if you're fighting for everything."

He scored fifteen goals that season, and five more for England, and he moved up to an incredible sixteen assists. He'd been put on set-plays, corners, free-kicks. He'd started the season uncertain and finished it main man. He won the club's Player of the Year and was runner-up in the national PFA Player of the Year and Football Writers' Footballer of the Year. But he still hadn't won anything with the team and the man who had stayed with him, manager Ranieri, was allowed to go.

"I loved him. He was a great man and a good manager. He did frustrate me when he wanted to change the team and change me, but I think he grew as a man in the job. I was a big signing for him at the time. He taught me a lot about my fitness, my life outside football, my discipline as a midfielder. He had an Italian way which wasn't easy for an English player, but he taught me many good things to take on.

"Winning the Chelsea Player of the Year was as important as winning any of the others at the time. That might sound cheesy, but I'd created this affair with the fans that was really special. I'd started achieving what I wanted to."

The Frank Lampard at Chelsea in 2004 when José Mourinho arrived was very different from the Frank Lampard who had walked into the club in 2001. Frank Lampard says so.

People talk about overseas players having to adapt to English culture and the Premier League. But thirty years ago they used to talk about Scottish players having to adapt when coming south. It would take a year, they said. In truth, moving from the East End of London to the West End can be a culture shock, even for a boy with a public school education like Lampard. He had got his ten GCSEs, he had enjoyed languages, he had retained his working-class background, he had not long come to terms with moving out of home, and yet had not been as ready as you'd believe or he believed for the short journey. Now he was ready for the biggest change yet in his life.

"My personality had completely strengthened. I became much tougher, much more worldly. I disappointed myself in that first year. I didn't feel I adapted to the bigger surroundings. West London, big players around me. I think for the second year I adapted more, I became much tougher."

For the fourth year, the targets were sky high. Asked early in his reign how he could improve Lampard, Mourinho replied: "I can help him become the best midfielder in the world." And that's what happened.

In time, Mourinho built his team around Frank Lampard and Didier Drogba. There were other crucial players, Cech, Terry and Makelele especially, but the attacking shape of the side was set out with a lone central striker because Drogba could do that on his own, and because it left gaps for Lampard to burst through. In Lampard's fourth season, Chelsea won the League with a record number of points. He scored nineteen goals, managed an unbelievable thirty-one assists, and played in fifty-eight games.

"Everything clicked. I felt a huge player at the club along with John. He got PFA Player of the Year and I got Footballer of the Year. We became deadly at set-pieces that year, JT in particular. Mourinho put me on every set-piece almost, me or one of the left-footers.

"That 'best midfielder in the world' was typical of what Mourinho would say behind closed doors. After two weeks he said to me: 'You're the best player in the world, you've just got to win something.' He made me believe. For me, he is the most magnificent man manager. He's made me what I am.

"He never particularly tactically improved me, he never really told me anything. He just said: 'You need to be a winner, then you'll be World Player of the Year.' He improved my head. He made me believe what he believed. That's special!"

When Mourinho found his Chelsea shape of 4-3-3, Lampard became unstoppable. In front of a four-man defence, Makelele was the midfield anchor. A reliable all-round midfielder took the right side – Tiago or Smertin – although later the more attacking Gudjohnsen was moved there, and Lampard was free on the left. Ahead, Drogba marauded through the middle with a winger either side from Duff, Robben and Joe Cole. Sometimes Gudjohnsen, more withdrawn, was in the middle up front which gave Lampard still more licence to attack.

"Four-three-three gave me an even freer role," he purrs. "Maka was very disciplined, the other midfielder more disciplined than I had to be. I built a tactical awareness of getting into more attacking positions, between lines, between defenders. Mourinho wanted me to dominate from there.

"Also, I enjoyed cutting in from that inside-left position, hitting long-range shots." The goals and set-ups came thick and fast. By January Chelsea were shoe-ins to win their first title in fifty years. By February they had won the Carling Cup against Liverpool, Lampard's first trophy.

Ten days later Chelsea beat Barcelona 4-2 at Stamford

Bridge to progress to the quarter-final of the Champions League. He made it 2-0 on the night. "That was probably the best all-round game I've been involved in. The first twenty minutes was sheer pleasure." Chelsea went 3-0 up in that time. "To beat a team of Barcelona's ability! I'll never forget the manager running on at the end and giving me a hug and the two of us walking to the Matthew Harding Stand end. We were on a different level by then."

In the quarter-final Chelsea won the first leg 4-2 at home to Bayern Munich. Lampard scored twice, and his second goal was one of the finest seen at the ground. Makelele chipped the ball to him, his chest control was not great, but as the ball lobbed over his head he turned and struck a left-footed half volley into the far corner of the net with amazing power, speed and accuracy. "I was in a rich vein of form. That's in my best two goals for Chelsea."

He means the best two in quality. The best two in emotion were to come a few weeks later. Chelsea finally landed the title away to Bolton with a 2-0 win. He bagged both goals.

"That was probably the best day of my life! My two kids being born, and that! The best three days! The goose bumps I get still watching those goals! Someone phoned me later when Eidur and I were in the hotel watching *Match Of The Day* and said you don't know what you've done for Chelsea fans, you've made history!

"One of the best things was my mum and dad were in the crowd, I couldn't get them directors' box tickets, and they said it was amazing to be there. Imagine celebrating with the fans seeing your boy score two goals and win the League!"

In the final game of the season he scored the equaliser in a 1-1 draw at Newcastle. The first thing he checked with me afterwards was the statistics. "Nineteen goals, that beat Poyet's eighteen, right?" It was right. He gave a little punch of the air. Lampard had to be best. He had to be the winner.

He became only the second Chelsea player, following Gianfranco Zola, to be named Footballer of the Year. His speech, during which he talked about his role as a patron to the Teenage Cancer Trust, an activity which had started to become increasingly important to him, was received to massive acclaim from the journalists. At the end of 2005 he was second to Ronaldinho in both European Player of the Year and World Player of the Year. He was voted into the first FifPro XI, the players' union team voted for around the world, and for the second year running he was made England Player of the Year by the national team's fans.

"I got a lot of accolades," he admits with pride, "but the World Player of the Year was massive. Second to Ronaldinho, who is an absolute genius. It was a special night to stand up between him and Eto'o." Samuel Eto'o, like Ronaldinho a member of the Barcelona team Lampard and Chelsea had defeated, was third. "I was very proud!"

Chelsea went and did it again the next season, back-to-back titles. He hit twenty goals this time. He got twenty-one assists. He broke the Premier League record of consecutive appearances in games, taking it to 164 before illness robbed him of extending the record. Such attacking prowess in a midfielder couldn't be one-way only, 'forward gears and no reverse' as Dennis Wise used to describe it, when Chelsea's defence was so tight. He did his defending too.

Yet perhaps the world began to take his extraordinary feats for granted. There was no way he could keep to the same level without periods of less brilliance. Whenever those occurred people said he was tired with all the games. That was rubbish. Then, when opposition came up with the brilliant idea of man-marking Makelele, he found his anchor moving away from the centre and he had to fill in. The balance wasn't quite the same and his game did suffer. Chelsea had the title wrapped up even earlier this year, and the competitive edge of the team blunted in the second half of the campaign.

He followed the season with a goalless World Cup, and football fans around the nation began to turn on him. He is philosophical about the process, especially given it included some more of the most glorious days of his career.

"I don't think Chelsea fans, or people in the club, took me for granted, but I think outside people did. It's the typical English thing. What more could I do? You do the same and people put you down. We won the League again. I was the first player in the country to get ten Premiership goals, ahead of all the strikers. To be fair, my form dipped around Christmas. But it was another great season.

"The 164 League games is something I'm really proud of now. I wasn't that bothered at the time. But I was upset when I broke down at Manchester City, and then when I considered what it spanned, two managers, a new owner, it was something very special. It'll be hard for it to be done again by an outfield player."

Among his special moments that year was a penalty in front of the Kop to put Chelsea one-up against Liverpool at Anfield. "We won 4-1 in front of the Kop. It was a great moment, the Liverpool-Chelsea rivalry had started. Liverpool fans had a bit of a vendetta against me, they thought that I was trying to prise Gerrard to come south and play with me." Also, finally, after almost five years, he scored his first goal against West Ham, away at his old home ground. "That was very pleasing. I deserved that. My family were there for that too."

And almost a year on from his great day, same ground, same goal, same corner of the goal, almost the same · outcome, he scored in a 2-0 win at Bolton. "It was the same everything. It was a sweet moment to be scoring in the same spot again. We didn't win the Premier League that day but we were almost there."

Following on, his sixth Chelsea season was more of the

same. Unbelievably, he bettered his goalscoring, twenty-one goals this time, twenty-one more assists, and although it didn't turn out to be a third consecutive title, winning the FA Cup as well as another Carling Cup established another top season. The World Cup hangover simply didn't exist for him.

"When I came home from the World Cup I felt like people outside Chelsea wanted to follow that through. My main concern was focusing on Chelsea. I knew I wouldn't get the same stick as outside. It turned out to be a very difficult season with the club, but fortunately Didi became an absolute phenomenon." Didier Drogba scored thirty-three goals. "I was very pleased for him, he had started to take some stick. He's a great guy, an honest fella who speaks his mind, physically he's awesome, and he become the best striker in the world. I looked for him, his movement, his pace and power, and I loved playing with him."

The team suffered from injuries but still battled on to be fighting for all four trophies at the beginning of May. Lampard was putting together more appearances in one season than any player in Chelsea history, sixty-four.

The side also suffered from a change of shape. Mourinho had gone to 4-4-2 with a midfield diamond. That protected Makelele and brought in established stars like Michael Ballack and Andriy Shevchenko. But the team stuttered, the new boys struggled, and it was left to Lampard and Drogba to supply the main attacking play. At Barcelona in the Group stage of the Champions League, Lampard produced his favourite goal in a 2-2 draw. Again he found himself chasing a Makelele pass, reached the goal-line, turned, and with everyone expecting him to cross he fashioned a vicious chip beyond goalkeeper Victor Valdés and in off the far post.

If it had been Ronaldinho scoring, the media and the football world would have been wild in its praise. But now doubters claimed this was a cross, not a deliberate shot. Lampard's pride, his work, his belief, they all make him very angry when his peaks are not recognised.

"It rankled with me when people said I didn't mean it," he says, and he is frowning still with frustration. It's that pain at the thought of failure again. "That's my best Chelsea goal because of the angle, the accuracy, and if I did that one thousand times again I probably wouldn't score it."

He used to play a game after training, along with several other players, of putting a ball five to ten yards behind the goal-line and curling it into the goal. This strike was actually the technical perfection of a post-training competition between players.

In February 2007 he lifted his first major trophy. Terry was carried off with what looked a dreadful head injury during the course of the Carling Cup Final, and he received the trophy after the 2-1 victory over Arsenal at the Millennium Stadium.

"That was a strange game. I hit the woodwork from a long way out, and Didi was special again, coming up with the two goals. People might have thought we should have beaten that young Arsenal team anyway, but football doesn't always work out like that. Anyone who knows me knows I'm not concerned with lifting trophies. Of course, I enjoyed lifting it, but I'd have preferred John hadn't got injured and he'd lifted it. It was a worrying moment although we'd won."

Chelsea became only the third team to win the domestic Cup double that May, scooping the first trophy back at new Wembley. In extra time against Manchester United in the FA Cup Final, he supplied the one-touch pass for Drogba to score the winner.

"I was pleased with that. Didi was immense, absolutely player of the year. But that game was so massive after losing the League to them. Make no mistake, we'd have won that League without our injuries. It was such a huge thing for the English lads who had grown up seeing finals at Wembley.

Even having been through winning the Premier League twice, when you stood there and lifted the FA Cup you just didn't want to leave the pitch. Me and JT were hugging it on the pitch.

"Then Elen went and had our second baby the next day. That was a weekend-and-a-half! I was still half-pissed!"

In what seemed no time at all, Lampard was moving to one hundred goals for the club. He was just the eighth player to achieve that and, obviously, the first midfielder. He was moving towards four hundred games. He was achieving heights, longevity, the lot.

During 2007 he hit two hat-tricks, in the FA Cup against Macclesfield Town and in the Carling Cup against Leicester City. "It's a good achievement for a midfield player," he says with that relaxed pride. "I'd been on the verge of a hat-trick in so many games and never quite managed it."

Towards the end of the year he came up with another kind of a hat-trick: three assists for the first three goals as Chelsea beat fourth-placed Manchester City 6-0. The second, a technically extraordinary pass with the outside of his right boot for - no surprise - Drogba, was his finest defence-splitter yet.

"I think that was probably my best game for Chelsea," he says. It's a surprise. After all, the ace midfield goalscorer didn't score in this one. "Goals would have been the icing on the cake, and sometimes you score and people say you've played brilliantly when you haven't. But that game people said I'd played brilliantly and I didn't score. It was right up there with the best."

It is performances like this which make him dismiss lazy talk as to whether he can play with Ballack for Chelsea or Gerrard for England as rubbish. He points out: "I have different games. Sometimes I play deep, sometimes I push right up, and I don't think it's got any connection to the goals I score. Ranieri told me that. Sometimes I lie deep and arrive late there, and I started scoring more when I was doing that."

There is only one thing you can guarantee Frank Lampard won't go on to do. He won't become a veteran midfielder who drops to the anchor position to see out his days. His self-belief, his drive, his focus, never ticked that box. When he can't burst from deep anymore, when he can't win games, he'll bow out. And you'll be hard pushed to find a midfielder at the top level of the game anywhere in the world who will have won more games than Frank Lampard.

He looks back on his Chelsea career to date and feels the need to thank a lot of people.

Ken Bates
"I found him really interesting. He forked out the money to buy me, and then he took to me, and I took to him and his missus, Suzannah. They took me out to dinner. He was a person who was hated by some, but I found him interesting company. I enjoyed being with him."

Claudio Ranieri
"He gave me a much more worldly look on football."

José Mourinho
"Him, most of all, for giving me the confidence to go the highest level."

Roman Abramovich
"We would never have got anywhere near where we have without his intervention, and he helped us all, supported us all individually."

Team-mates

"I played in great teams with great spirit at Chelsea. There's never been any rancour. Everyone helped me settle, and I've had great players around me. Obviously JT, as captain and vice-captain we've been massively involved together. People like Jody Morris helped me settle when I first came, and he was a really good player on the pitch. Eidur was possibly my closest friend at the club in the time he was here. There's Maka for our relationship on the pitch. And Billy McCulloch (masseur) for keeping me fit for those 164 games, and keeping me entertained."

José Mourinho on Frank Lampard

"I don't see how he can improve because for me he is the best player in the world. I would not change Lampard for another player because he does everything. His defence is incredible, he can pass over a long distance, he can pass short. He can score over long distance. How can he improve?"

Frank Arnesen, Chelsea director of youth development

"I would never advise a young player to watch Frank Lampard and base his game on him. He is unique. No-one else could come from so deep so often and score so many goals. You can't learn that."

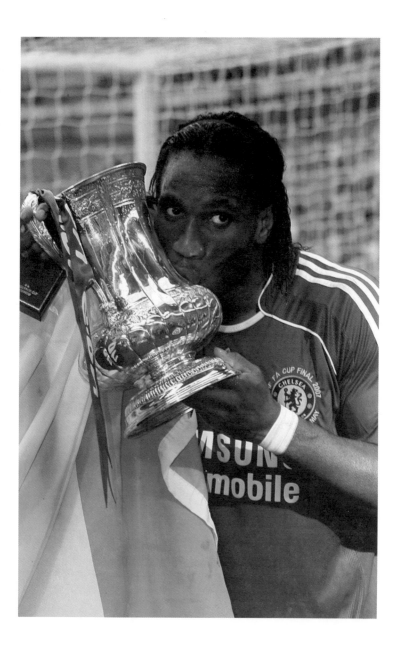

EARLY LAST WORD

Perfect
10

There are two people who need special mention at this point.
One made himself the best striker in the world. The other is
'The Special One.'

At the beginning of 2008 Didier Drogba was voted fourth in
the FIFA World Player of the Year poll for 2007. He was the
existing Africa Player of the Year. The three voted ahead of him
were not strikers: Kaká, Cristiano Ronaldo and Lionel Messi.

In his few years at the club Drogba had grown to become a
centre-forward with Peter Osgood's influence on the team. If
one season were to be selected as a measure of Chelsea's
Top Ten, then Drogba's 2006-07 season would place him firmly
near the top. He scored 33 goals, he scored some of the best
goals in the history of the club against the best teams the club
has ever played: his left-footed half-volley on the turn against
Liverpool, having chested the ball into space; his half-volley
after reverse-passing the ball to himself against Barcelona; his
40-yard volley to win the game at Everton; his two goals
against Arsenal to win the Carling Cup final at the Millennium
Stadium; his brilliant one-two with Lampard to score the only
goal of the first FA Cup Final back at Wembley against
Manchester United…

He made goals, he led the line, he closed opponents down,
he defended heroically at set-plays. He geed up the crowd,
almost Dennis Wise-style. In a season when the team

struggled in comparison to its two previous title-winning seasons, he kept the side going on four fronts to the beginning of May. He played in sixty games for Chelsea that season. It was an awesome performance.

Top scorers in a Chelsea season

Jimmy Greaves	43 (Division 1, 1960-61)
Bobby Tambling	37 (Division 2, 1962-63)
Jimmy Greaves	37 (Division 1, 1958-59)
Kerry Dixon	36 (Division 1, 1984-85)
Kerry Dixon	34 (Division 2, 1983-84)
Bob Whittingham	34 (Division 2, 1910-11)
Didier Drogba	33 (Premier League, 2006-07)
Peter Osgood	31 (Division 1, 1971-72)
Peter Osgood	31 (Division 1, 1969-70)
Jimmy Greaves	30 (Division 1, 1959-60)
Tommy Lawton	30 (Division 1, 1946-47)
Hughie Gallacher	30 (Division 1, 1931-32)
Bob Turnbull	30 (Division 2, 1925-26)
George Hilsdon	30 (Division 1, 1907-08)

'The Special One' never played for Chelsea. But if you were to have the Top Ten Stars, he would be at the very top. For José Mourinho is a superstar.

Arriving in 2004 after winning the Champions League with FC Porto, on the back of Chelsea having not won the title for forty-nine years and also on the back of manager Claudio Ranieri playing down any chances of Chelsea winning anything, he announced: "I believe I am a special one," and said that with the players he was inheriting Chelsea should win the title.

An overseas player arriving is supposed to need time to adapt. This overseas manager forced everyone in England to adapt to him. He was front-page news. His strong, good looks demanded photographs and broadcasting footage, his controversial sound-bites demanded headlines, his humour demanded attention and repetition, and his team won the title with a record number of points. Then they won it again.

In three years his team won six trophies, and to prove it he held up six fingers in the Royal Box at Wembley as he collected his FA Cup winners' medal. He was the greatest winner the club has ever had.

But he wasn't someone who basked in the good times and looked for cover in the bad. He led from the front. When Chelsea finally relinquished the title in his third season, at Arsenal following a brave 1-1 draw, he strode across the pitch to the Chelsea fans, demanded applause for the players, and then gave a chin-up gesture which was to be the image of the rest of the season. Manchester United fans tried to goad Chelsea fans with it before the FA Cup Final. Chelsea players all replied with it after winning.

Mourinho was everything: man manager, tactician, coach, organiser, leader. His tactical changes in a game were in advance of anyone else in the world. He was a genius. But with genius, you get edge. He was constantly in trouble with authority, he believed he could never be wrong, and in the end the authority which he couldn't handle or beat was his own boss, owner Roman Abramovich.

The truth almost certainly is that however negative headlines can be, fans like to wake up with their club being in the limelight, especially when it's front-page news as well as back. Mourinho gave Chelsea top billing everywhere. Perhaps Chelsea was guilty of failing to manage the top manager. It is one of the great sadnesses in the history of the club that they parted company after a little over three years. The West London swagger was made for José. The club will continue to miss his qualities massively. The fans miss him massively. And, forever, he will miss the club massively.

The José Mourinho era, 2004-2007

February 2005
>   Won the League Cup, the first Chelsea trophy since 2000.

April 2005
>   Reached the semi-final of the Champions League.
>   Won the Premier League, the first top-flight title since 1955.

May 2005
>   Completed the Premier League season with a record number of points.
>   Completed the Premier League season with a record low of goals conceded.

August 2005
>   Won the FA Community Shield.

April 2006
>   Won the Premier League again.

May 2006
>   Completed the Premier League season with the third-highest points total ever.

August 2006
>   FA Community Shield runners-up.

February 2007
>   League Cup winners again.

April 2007
>   Reached the semi-final of the Champions League again.

May 2007
>   Premier League runners-up.
>   FA Cup winners.

August 2007
>   FA Community Shield runners-up again.

Go out there, a Chelsea boy and try my nuts off

Joe
Cole

Joe Cole's mum is from a family of Chelsea supporters. He had Chelsea drummed into him as a youngster. His own interest in football was wider than that, but Chelsea was always number one in his heart.

In 1994, on the last day of the Premier League season, he was a ballboy at Stamford Bridge. Chelsea came from behind with two late Mark Stein goals to beat Sheffield United 3-2 and relegate them. The following week Chelsea were in the FA Cup Final for the first time in twenty-four years. At the end of the Stamford Bridge game there was a friendly pitch invasion. Joe, who had to head for the tunnel anyway, ran with the fans across the pitch rather than around it and finished up getting a straight-arm tackle from a steward.

"That's probably what made me join West Ham", he laughs.

He went to the '94 and 1997 FA Cup Finals as a guest of Chelsea but, however much the club tried to sign the much sought-after youngster, he wasn't going to join. Instead, he had to be bought from relegated West Ham United, still aged twenty-one, in the first summer of Roman Abramovich for £6.6m. He was the obvious successor to the line of sublime ball talent that had run through Charlie Cooke, Pat Nevin and Gianfranco Zola.

"I felt like I was coming home," he says of his 2003 move. But it didn't work out like that. He had to fight to be at home.

Immediately after signing he was taken down to the *Chelsea TV* offices where I was live on air. We put on a short video, rushed him into the studio where he swapped places with guest Graham Rix, who warmly shook his hand and told him he would be a massive success at Chelsea, and then he spoke in a way I hadn't expected.

He didn't want to talk about ball skills, magic, fantasy, being a Chelsea supporter or any of that. He just wanted to say that he was someone who gave one hundred per cent every game, and that is what Chelsea fans should expect.

Oh, the old clichés! Except that, in his case, it turned out to be the absolute truth. Joe Cole's skills are only one part of his game. He has an enormous engine – a unique one. He never stops working and as a rule covers more ground than almost anyone else on the pitch. For instance, his kilometres per game are normally higher than any other player when he completes ninety minutes – often he'll be half-a-kilometre up on his nearest rival.

He believes now that it is this attitude, even more than his skills, which has endeared him to Chelsea fans.

"There's no better judge of football than the fans," he claims. "Pundits or whatever might watch you two or three times a season. Fans know just as much. And many of them watch every game. They know I give my all. That's why they took to me. I'm not like a Thierry Henry, I'm Joe. Go out there, a Chelsea boy, and try my nuts off every game.

"I feel like I'm at home now. I have to stay here the rest of my career!"

He's right! He is Joe! For this book's interview we have met in the Health Club at Stamford Bridge. It's the day after a game, and he was training in the morning at Cobham where the club's facilities are based. He chose not to eat in Cobham's excellent canteen.

At the Health Club he chooses burger and potato wedges for his lunch. It's a proper burger, not a junk one, but it's the food of his roots. He'd prefer the wedges to be a bit crisper. Or, to put it bluntly, a bit more oily! Fuel for his running! Food he can enjoy.

Not only were there barriers to Joe Cole establishing himself with Chelsea when he was a youngster, but again with Claudio Ranieri when he was signing, and once more with José Mourinho when he was maturing. The Joe Cole story really is yet another Chelsea one against the odds.

He dismisses media reports that the reason he signed for West Ham was money.

"There was a lot in the media saying Joe is getting twenty grand a week and that kind of thing. It was absolute rubbish. We were offered things by clubs, but my dad said he wouldn't sell his son, he'll go where he wants to go.

"My dad ran a fruit and veg stall, and agents were phoning offering all sorts of things. But West Ham was where I felt most comfortable. I had a lot of friends there. They had the best young players, and I saw a way into the first team. Even from a young age I was very focused.

"I came and played for Chelsea as a youngster, I remember playing against Spurs at U11s or U12s, but West Ham felt right. Chelsea was a bit run down then. I loved getting the tickets for the first team, but there were not enough good players around. I was thinking 'where can I improve?' Everything has changed now!"

The decision seemed to be quickly justified. When he was seventeen he starred in the FA Youth Cup-winning team which beat Coventry City 9 0 on aggregate in the final. Goalkeeper Stephen Bywater and his close friend Michael Carrick were colleagues in the West Ham side. Chris Kirkland kept goal for Coventry. There were a good crop of players around.

The following season he was increasingly involved in the first team. But although the English media was talking him up, playing top-class football wasn't easy.

"I was playing above my age when I was at school, but even up to 19-years-old when I'd played 50, 60, 70 games for the first team, I was so slight. I'm a stone heavier now. I didn't have the pace to get by anyone. I was a very late developer. Because of what I could do with the ball people said I'd be playing at sixteen in the first team, but physically and mentally I wasn't up to scratch. I got by on technique alone.

"Then the summer before the 2002 World Cup I came back putting on weight, and people said that it was pre-season that had built me up. But it wasn't, I'd just had a late growth spurt. Suddenly I could get by people for the first time since the youth team. And that's when I started playing wide."

His best position has remained a debate amongst football folk. Central midfield, the hole behind two forwards, alone behind one forward, wide in a midfield four, wide in a front three, one of a midfield three? Where best can he display his skills? Is there a position which demands too much responsibility and forces him to blunt his skills?

He's still open-minded. "I'd played in the middle of a 4-4-2, that's where I had most success at West Ham. I'd played wide, and in my last season I played the holding midfield position as well. And I was capable there. When my old legs go I think I'll go back to that holding role! Play there until I'm God knows how old!"

He was also captain of West Ham in his last season. So it was a 21-year-old with a lot of experience, an international who had already scored for England, who joined Chelsea and the whirlwind revolution in 2003. His battles at the Bridge were to be very different from those in East London.

In the 2006-07 season Joe suffered a knee injury in

pre-season and had started only two games when he was diagnosed with a stress fracture of the foot in November. He required surgery and came off crutches in mid-February. When he was finally able to walk freely again, he dribbled a ball indoors wherever he went, from the training ground changing room to the medical room, from the rehabilitation room to the canteen.

It brought to mind stories that as a child he used to go to bed with a football. Stories, he happily reports, which are true.

"When I was a kid, all the time I used to think that if I didn't play football everyday I wouldn't make it as a footballer. If I woke up feeling ill I wouldn't tell my mother, 'cause if I couldn't go to school I couldn't play football. So I went to school for two hours, and if I was too ill to play with friends I'd keep the ball and just kick up myself, do tricks and so on. And then I'd have to admit how ill I was and go home.

"If I went to visit family friends at weekends or during the holidays, I'd get home at night and make my dad stand there and I'd dribble round him in the dark. I'm still like that now. If I don't train one hundred per cent, I feel like I won't perform in games."

When he finally signed for Chelsea in 2003, the circumstances turned out not to have improved on the 1990s. Chelsea was wealthier, stronger, but it seemed to him in a muddle.

Gianfranco Zola had been allowed to leave that summer – in a muddle. Despite being 37-years-old he had just been voted Player of the Year and was top scorer as Chelsea qualified for the Champions League for the first time since 1999. But the club was broke and Zola was at the end of his contract. There were young forwards like Carlton Cole and Mikael Forssell who would be a lot cheaper to maintain. The Italian wasn't offered a new contract.

By the time Roman Abramovich had bought the club, Zola

had agreed to move to Cagliari. It was a word of mouth agreement, but he felt he couldn't go back on it, so no matter how much Chelsea tried, the player fans voted the best in the club's history was lost.

Who would take his place? If it was to be Joe Cole, that wasn't obvious to the player himself in his dealings with manager Claudio Ranieri.

"When I signed I met him in a hotel in Hertfordshire, and Chelsea had just played a friendly and you could tell he didn't want to be there. I kept asking what position he'd play me, and he kept saying: 'You are my key, you open the door.'

"A lot of the big clubs were in for me, Manchester United and Arsenal were making noises – it was supposed to be Verón to Chelsea and me to United – there was interest from Barcelona and Valencia, but nothing concrete, and Chelsea was the first team to make a bid. It was such an opportunity to come and play for the team I'd supported, but Claudio didn't inspire me. I thought if I just go there he'll have to play me, I'll show him how good I am.

"But then when I turned up at Chelsea to sign, Verón was sitting there next to me! I thought they must be buying a job lot of midfielders!

"I'd asked Claudio if I could play in the No. 10 shirt. I'd always dreamt to play No. 10 for Chelsea. I was just about to sign and Trevor (Birch, chief executive) said to my dad: 'What about shirt No. 20 or 16?' My dad said that I'd been promised No. 10. But apparently that was being given to Seba (Verón).

"My dad said to me: 'B*******, come on, let's go! If they promise you something they've got to do it.' To be honest, I was going to accept it, but he said it was the principle. Anyway, Claudio rang Seba and he said that it was no problem, so it all got sorted."

Cole soon discovered the difference between world superstar Verón and 'I'm Joe.'

"We went to the first press conference. Seba had an entourage all in suits. I turned up in a tracksuit or jeans or something by myself. He was the big news, this massive Argentine player I looked up to, and we were probably competing for the same position."

Ranieri described Verón as the best midfielder in the world at that press conference. Verón responded by describing Joe as the best midfielder in England. In the end the two rarely competed for the same position. In fact, neither played very much.

The first game was a Champions League Group qualifier in Zilina in Slovakia. Joe came off the bench after 69 minutes to substitute the summer record signing, £17m Damien Duff, on the left-wing. It hadn't been a job lot of midfielders purchased in 2003. It had been a team! Goalkeepers Neil Sullivan, Marco Ambrosio and Jürgen Macho; full-backs Glen Johnson and Wayne Bridge; midfielders Gérémi, Verón, Claude Makelele, Duff and Cole; and forwards Hernán Crespo and Adrian Mutu.

Six minutes into his debut Cole helped set up Chelsea's second goal. It was typical Joe Cole play. He received the ball from a throw-in near the halfway line, played a diagonal ball forward to centre-forward Eidur Gudjohnsen and made a diagonal run. He got the return, fed it back again, kept going, got another return, stopped and back-heeled it to still-running Gudjohnsen. This time the striker's touch wasn't so good but defender Drahno, in trying to intercept, chipped the ball over his own goalkeeper and into the net. Chelsea won 2-0.

Joe still has mixed feelings about the occasion. "I was sitting there after the game getting a rub, and Claudio comes up and says: 'See, you are my key.' I thought: 'Oh yeah, that's it, coming off the bench!' But it was a good start."

There was to be a lot of coming off the bench that season. There was to be a lot of not even making the bench. He stayed belligerently full of confidence.

"I had to bed in. I had a lot to prove, but the fans took to me straight away." They gave him a song immediately about being here, there and everywhere, the old Frank Lebœuf song (lyrics not repeatable here), but perhaps more suitably a song first used for Charlie Cooke.

"I wasn't having big games, but I felt on top of my game. I didn't score many but I created a few. It didn't seem to matter if I played well and created a goal, others were picked ahead of me next game. It took me to the end of the season when Claudio gave me six games on the spin, and I think that's when my Chelsea career started – more than when José came. Until then I'd thought I was putting my head against a brick wall with him."

Defeat in the first leg of the Champions League semi-final in Monaco resulted in Joe being promoted to the starting eleven, and he played in the second leg at home. "That was a big game for me, but I was so disappointed at how it ended. I still think we would have won it that year if it hadn't been for the circumstances in Monaco. I think the manager's got to take the responsibility.

"Me, Jimmy (Floyd Hasselbaink) and Seba were on the bench, Seba had been out for five months, and he shoves him on (at half-time for Jesper Grønkjær). Seba couldn't believe it. I think that cost us the Champions League."

Monaco came back from 2-0 down at Stamford Bridge to draw 2-2, but lost the final to Porto – who were managed by José Mourinho. That summer, Mourinho moved to Chelsea. Joe was to discover he had another barrier to jump.

"He is a good boy," said José Mourinho in January 2005. "For me he is a completely different player. Instead of being sad and speaking to you (the press), when he is sad he wants to improve."

In late 2006 Terry Venables, at the time England's assistant coach, said: "He's a player who's improved every year."

Four goals, between August 21st 2004 and January 1st 2005, were crucial in Joe Cole's changing fortunes. They were all as substitute. It said something unique for his temperament at the time.

Joe didn't make Mourinho's first two starting line-ups. He didn't make the bench for the first game. The manager went with a midfield diamond, Frank Lampard being at the top behind the forwards, and Gérémi and Alexei Smertin on the sides. It was solid, compact, but not penetrating.

Chelsea won the first game 1-0 and were drawing 0-0 at Birmingham City in the second when Mourinho changed things. Cole was his final substitution following two at half-time. With 68 minutes gone he was sent on for Gérémi and the team was switched to 4-3-3. He played up front on the left-wing. Ten minutes later he scored.

Cutting in purposefully from the flank he left behind former team-mate Mario Melchiot, then Birmingham's right-back, and swept a shot which deflected off central defender Martin Taylor. Chelsea won 1-0 again. He held down his place for a while, but a fit-again Damien Duff soon took it over.

When Liverpool went to Stamford Bridge at the beginning of October he was back on the bench. He replaced an injured Didier Drogba before half-time, playing on the right of the front three this time. The only goal of the game was just past the hour when his bright run took him ahead of his set-play marker Luis Garcia, and he turned in Lampard's free-kick.

After the game the media was full of him, but not Mourinho. The manager lambasted his performance following the goal and said it wasn't good enough, and neither was his attitude. He had to learn to defend, to play for the team and to stop playing for the gallery – doing tricks in the wrong places. Next game he was back on the bench.

He started once more at West Bromwich Albion at the end of the month, but after a first half in which Chelsea led 1-0 despite being poor, Mourinho turned up in the dressing room, posted two substitutions on the wall, and Cole was off again. He didn't figure in the Premier League for another two months.

He was now at his lowest point. But his mind didn't falter.

"I wasn't leaving Chelsea without proving I could be a success. There was no way I was leaving as a failure. I was already seeing a lot of big players come and go. It was important it wasn't me.

"I didn't want to start complaining, but it wasn't a great thing that happened to me, and then in that two months out Duffa and (Arjen) Robben were playing really well. José didn't believe in me from the off. But I believed in myself. It was very rare I didn't put a performance in. What made things worse, in the two months when I was out of the team I lost my nan, and that really affected me. We were very close. It was the hardest time of my life, not just my career.

"But I came out of that, and all of a sudden things fell for me on the pitch."

How they fell!

Between Christmas and New Year he returned off the bench at Portsmouth after 72 minutes, replacing Smertin with the score at 0-0. Chelsea won 2-0, and he scored the second in stoppage time, a twenty-yard left-footer. Three days later he replaced Duff with fifteen minutes remaining in the crucial clash at Anfield on New Year's Day. After five minutes he drove the only goal of the game from a corner which was knocked down to him. Liverpool 0 Chelsea 1. In his post-match press conference Mourinho said with some enthusiasm that Joe Cole now deserved his chance.

Two weeks later Mourinho claimed: "For me he is a completely different player," as Joe started in the Premier

League for the first time in three months. "I keep saying to him you do not have to show your talent because everyone knows that. I need you to show me you can think through the tactical points of view."

On February 1st Arjen Robben suffered a metatarsal break. After a short tussle he won the vacant spot ahead of Gudjohnsen and proceeded to play all the big games. He went from being a crowd favourite to a top player. So 2005 was a great year. As was the first half of 2006.

Much credit went to Mourinho from the media for the improvement in Cole's consistency and efficacy. But the player is more temperate in his praise.

"He deserves a small amount of credit, he's helped me as a footballer. But lots of people at Chelsea do. It was only a small brick – he'll say that himself – and it would be wrong to single out him and not single out my parents and coaches at West Ham and elsewhere. Over the years you get what you deserve.

"Peter Brabrook (a former Chelsea player with 271 appearances) was my coach at West Ham from eleven to fourteen, and he had a massive impact on my football. I still speak to him now, he works with my dad and he's a lovely fella. Jimmy Hampson was the youth development officer at West Ham and he helped me with off the field stuff. Then there was Keith Blunt with the FA, Glenn Roeder, Harry Redknapp, Sven (Gorän Eriksson), Steve McClaren…

"Imagine if I didn't score in those games! I might have been on the bench for another six months. A lot of what happened was because I was fighting against him. I made him play me! I think when he really wanted me was once I was injured. Don't get me wrong, I think ho's an amazing man. But I think if he believed in me more we could have won even more trophies!"

Two things helped Cole. Mourinho's preference to play him

as an attacking winger in a three was the first. "I think it suits me, 4-3-3, I can play inside as a midfield three or outside as a winger." The other thing was his engine which continued to impress the fans. He worked and worked.

Suddenly the good times came. He played in Barcelona in the Champions League, then won his first senior medal in the Carling Cup Final. He scored an unbelievable goal at Norwich City as Chelsea closed down on the title. He powered through a tackle and let rip from distance with his left foot, smashing the ball into the top corner. "That was a special finish, and it gave me a confidence factor going into the return against Barcelona. Finishing with my left from outside the penalty area...I'm not a Frank Lampard, but I watched him do it and I worked on it a lot."

Against Barcelona at home he was one of many shining stars as Chelsea won one of the finest games ever at Stamford Bridge 4-2. "I felt like I could run all night! I just felt amazing. It's one of the two best games I've played in, the other being a 5-4 at West Ham, which had everything the Barcelona game had plus comedy! The Barcelona game had a life of its own. I had no doubt we were going to win. And their team was probably the best team anywhere of the last ten years."

He'd made the second goal with a run which featured a trick to get inside Giovanni van Bronckhorst, followed by a shot the goalkeeper couldn't hold. Lampard put in the rebound. But even better was to follow against Bayern Munich. Chelsea won the first leg 4-2 again, and were leading 2-1 in Munich going into stoppage time. His performance in Munich was his best yet for the club.

"It was against a top side, and I squared the ball to Lamps for the first goal and made the second." That was his best assist of the year. He chased a long ball from Lampard to the left corner flag, leaving the opposition well behind. He lingered on the ball and, with only Drogba to pick out in the area, finally delivered a cross of exquisite precision which the centre-forward headed in.

"I love those big European nights. I enjoy the flow of European football better than Premier League football. That was a big game chasing (Bixente) Lizarazu and Zé Roberto all night. We had Huthy (Robert Huth) at right-back, out of position, so I had to look after him a little bit."

That was exactly what he did, and his defensive work received as much praise as his creative genius. Chelsea went on to win the Premier League, but lose the semi-final of the Champions League. Winning the title was a new climax for him.

"It meant everything. It was everything I had worked for as a player. I can remember the final whistle going at Bolton when we'd won it, but then the following week at home to Charlton when we were going to receive the trophy and medals and all of my family were watching, I went and got all emotional! I had to have a moment on my own at the end. I thought, 'don't start crying now you doughnut, you won the League last week.' That was so special!"

However, once again Cole started the following season on the bench as Chelsea beat Arsenal in the FA Community Shield. From behind the goal he joined in the celebrations as Didier Drogba put Chelsea two-up. His team spirit, he says, came naturally. "I'm a Chelsea supporter through and through, and no-one likes losing to Arsenal at anything. I'd back a Chelsea chess team against Arsenal!

"I was upset because I'd scored and made as many goals as Duff and Robben the last year. People were always talking about them. I was chokcd. I felt I deserved a little bit more respect from the manager. And now we had Wrighty as well."

Mourinho had signed Shaun Wright-Phillips, a fourth winger, for big money. But Cole was soon back in the team. He scored on his first start, of course, against West Bromwich Albion, and went on to have an outstanding campaign. It climaxed in the last home game of the season, a 3-0 win over Manchester United to win the title. He scored a goal of unique beauty. Receiving the ball twenty-five yards out with his back to goal, and with dexterous jiggery-pokery on it, turned Rio Ferdinand and stepped away from Mikael Silvestre before side-footing home.

"Again," he points out, "I'd been left out of the semi-final of the FA Cup the week before. You don't rotate players who are playing well! The gaffer went to a diamond for that and said the wingers were not playing well. I thought if ever someone's dropped I was the one to be out of the team. But against United was probably the best goal of my career, for the importance of the day, for it being against them, winning the League for the second time. I bloody nearly cried again! I'm quite an emotional person."

After that he received the praise he had perhaps been most yearning. "For the first time the manager sat me down and said you're one of my important players. I thought – that is *so* overdue!"

That summer he was arguably England's best player in a disappointing World Cup. "I really loved the World Cup. I established myself on the world stage. I scored a great goal. I swapped my shirt with one of their fellas after the game, and when I went in the dressing room JT (John Terry) said: 'Where's your shirt?' He said you can't give it away after that goal! So I went in the Sweden dressing room and got it back."

In the pre-season of 2006-07, when he was on top of his game, Joe Cole suffered a knee injury. So once again he missed the start of the season. As it turned out, he missed almost the whole season.

He came back in late October and scored on his first start, a

Carling Cup tie at Blackburn, and that earned him a substitute role at Barcelona in the Champions League once more. But by the end of November he was sidelined again, this time with a stress fracture of the foot. Chelsea had brought in big-name players, Michael Ballack and Andriy Shevchenko, but they hadn't adapted on the pitch and the football was a struggle.

Mourinho went mostly with a midfield diamond and increasingly lamented the loss of Cole.

He returned after a couple of substitute cameos at half-time in the second leg of the Champions League quarter-final when Chelsea were a goal down at Valencia, having drawn the first leg. He was outstanding as a 2-1 win was achieved.

He then played in the victorious FA Cup semi-final, and scored the only goal of the Champions League semi-final first leg at home to Liverpool. But his body wasn't right and he was fighting a long battle.

"I had one foot at the time! I had the pin in my foot and it wasn't properly healed. I was in a lot of pain. I could only play one game every ten days, but they were coming every three or four days and I just couldn't say no. It wasn't until the following pre-season, just a couple of days before the season really, that I played totally pain-free."

He proudly made the starting line-up for the 2007 FA Cup Final against Manchester United. "Yeah," he notes acidly, "and I got dragged off at half-time 'cause I wasn't magnificent. I felt I was doing well, our tactics were working. But I'm a Chelsea supporter, and I got another medal! It was very sweet when we won. That finished my England collection. Now I need the Champions League. The Daddy One!"

The 2007-08 pre-season wasn't an easy one either. He couldn't find the sharpness, the near year out seemed to have taken its toll, and he was out of the team again until just before Mourinho's departure in mid-September. After an uncertain start under new manager Avram Grant, the team won again in Valencia to launch a fine run of results. Once again Valencia took the lead. He equalised. Then he hit a glorious forty-yard pass with the outside of his foot for Didier Drogba to score the winner. Over the ninety minutes he also covered more ground than any other player on the pitch. Joe Cole was back to doing what he did best as a schoolkid and all through his career…making the difference while trying his nuts off.

So why does Joe Cole complete the Top Ten? Or, to be precise, why does he complete the 'Eight-And-Two-Halves-And-One-For-The-Future?'

It's a mixture of reasons: his qualities and achievements, his attitude, his relationship with the fans – how important has that been with each of the top players! – and equally importantly, how he can progress over the coming few years. He sees it in the same way.

"I like to play hard. If I didn't I might score and make more goals. But for me to be effective for the team I have to work both ways. It might not be twenty-five goals a season or twenty-five assists a season, but it's winning games! If that means shutting people down in the last five minutes, that's what I do. For me the greatest enjoyment is in winning games, winning trophies.

"I think there's more to come. I can be more consistent. I can play more. I haven't started a season for five years!

"You know, I've always had an itch to go to Spain and play for one of the big teams, but the more I get older the more I know how lucky I am to be playing at Chelsea. I want to stay here for the rest of my career. I want a big sackful of medals when I finish my career."

He's not doing badly now, I point out.

"I want more! And what I want most is the Champions League!"

Peter Brabrook, Chelsea contemporary of Jimmy Greaves, later a West Ham schoolboy and youth coach

"Joe Cole was the best schoolboy and youth player I've seen. He was better than Jimmy Greaves. Jimmy scored goals. Joe had more to his game. He was unbelievable on the ball. He did more tricks than Tommy Cooper. That goes away as you go up the levels, but he retained an element of it and still has it today."

Joe Cole on *Chelsea TV* at half-time in an FA Youth Cup match he was watching, talking about Chelsea prospect and ball skills specialist Gael Kakuta

"Yep, number eleven, the winger, he's a good player. I'll have to go home and do a few crunches if he keeps playing like that. Go and have an extra session! He's only 16, but yeah, looks a prospect."

THE FINAL WORD

Perfect
10

The final word goes, of course, to Chelsea owner Roman Abramovich. It is a silent one. Roman Abramovich does not talk in public.

Since buying Chelsea in 2003, he has spoken only by actions. They have fallen into three categories. Firstly, there's been his enthusiasm, his uninhibited passion screaming from every inch of his body as he watches his club play. The cheering, the groaning, the kicking every ball, the laughter, the high-fives, the in-and-out-of-his-seat half-jumping, the cheeks-in-his-hands one hundred per cent concentrating! That, more than anything, seems to have won over Chelsea fans.

Secondly, there's been his willingness to spend huge amounts of money. In his first summer he bought Duff, Crespo, Mutu, Makelele, Verón, Bridge, Joe Cole, Gérémi and Johnson. At Christmas he bought Parker. Football had never seen anything like it. And so it has gone on. That seems to have kept the fans pretty happy too!

Thirdly, there has been his silent insistence on getting his way. His inherited manager Ranieri went after one year of winning nothing. José Mourinho, the 'Special One', won six trophies in three years, but they fell out. Abramovich brought in his own people to bolster the business: Frank Arnesen to scout, Avram Grant to oversee. Mourinho left. Grant took over and took Chelsea to the Champions League Final. But then he was dispatched. Maybe the fans were concerned at how much hands-on say the owner was demanding.

The media tried to fill the void with stories of what Roman Abramovich was thinking or saying or doing. His every absence from games was a story. His presence at games was a story. The truth is the media had little idea of what he was thinking or how hands-on he was being, or even what he was doing. Work? Pleasure? How much time did he spend on either? The man was saying nothing. The media didn't know. With him, more than anyone, you could not believe what you read in the papers.

This is not the place to reveal private conversations or the thoughts of Roman Abramovich as addressed to me. But two small stories can leak into these pages.

After the departure of Mourinho, we were discussing his continued silence in the media. It seemed crazy to change the successful policy. After all, he had come to London big enough and wealthy enough not to have to play the media game, and especially the tabloids' game, and he had achieved an independence through doing that. True, it meant some of his beliefs and actions were distorted. But they would be distorted anyway. The argument I offered to him was: "If you get in bed with the British media, they will **** you!"

I expect silence for a long time.

Secondly, although I asked him for a formal interview for this book and received, as I expected, a polite refusal, he has privately already had a say. Some months before, when I told him what I was doing, like any fan he demanded to know who the Top Ten was, and then enthusiastically debated the rights and the wrongs of it. He had strong views. They didn't entirely agree with mine. Why should they! Beyond the banks, beyond the oil, steel and gold investments, beyond the houses and jets and boats, this multi-billionaire is like you and me.

There have been a lot of media reports about how Roman Abramovich wants entertaining football and loved the style of Barcelona when they were at their peak under the management of Frank Rijkaard. Who wouldn't love that!

It would also have been fair to say that he has been impressed with the play and style of Arsenal, and the way that club has been run in the past. So, it wasn't so far fetched for him to believe the unknown Avram Grant could turn out, on taking over from Mourinho at Chelsea, to be similar to the little known Arsène Wenger when he became manager at Arsenal.

Wenger quickly won trophies and stamped his personality on the club. When Grant failed to do either, Abramovich was not concerned about his own image if it meant moving Chelsea on. Grant was removed.

It would be fair to say, I believe, that Abramovich was impressed with the unique tactical acumen of Mourinho, with the trophies won, with the correct conducting of themselves by Arsenal, with the good balance of conduct, football and business by Manchester United. To want entertainment, silverware and also popularity for the way you act in your work may seem a lot to ask, but if you start off by demanding anything less then surely you are being unambitious and irresponsible. However, to seek it to the ultimate suddenly makes you appear ruthless, at least in the English media. That was probably difficult for Abramovich to understand. All he was trying to do was create the kind of club that you or I would want to create.

He is, by nature, a listener. He asks questions. He wants to hear the answers. He doesn't expect to hear what he is supposed to hear. He wants to learn, assess, conclude. Then he will have the final word.

And so he talks with people, many people, and in that sense is perhaps more hands-on than many realise. People talk directly to him regularly. Not just the manager and the chief executive, but the chief medical officer Bryan English, the director of youth development and head of scouting Arnesen, and the club captain John Terry. Many more are in regular contact through his confidante, club director Eugene Tenenbaum. More people have been added to the Chelsea backroom team to support the structure – some with the managers' enthusiasm, others not. The medical department has mushroomed. Chelsea is big, big business.

Of course, it is a different football club to what it was before he bought it. Of course there is a greater business activity going on, the whole show is more 'Hollywood', turnover as well as costs have multiplied, and the higher costs have meant more money being spent by many fans to continue following the team. It has meant a significant minority can no longer afford to attend regularly. It is a tragedy that old die-hard supporters have fallen by the wayside. However, that is true at all big clubs. Chelsea are not the most expensive club to watch in the Premier League, and offer good deals on Cup games which bring in new support and attract back old supporters. There have been positive away arrangements on travel and tickets offered as well as big demands on wallets. In other words, the picture is a complex one, and so it is with Abramovich's input.

The hardest part of fulfilling his ambitions is that he and Chelsea are playing catch-up with the biggest clubs in Europe, and those clubs have men with cute minds running them.

Take Manchester United. In Abramovich's first year at Chelsea, Arsenal won the League unbeaten, Chelsea came second and United only third. But United won the FA Cup. In his second year, Chelsea were first, Arsenal second and United again third. They won nothing. That summer Malcolm Glazer, the American sports tycoon, won control of United and there was widespread speculation that the debt he was

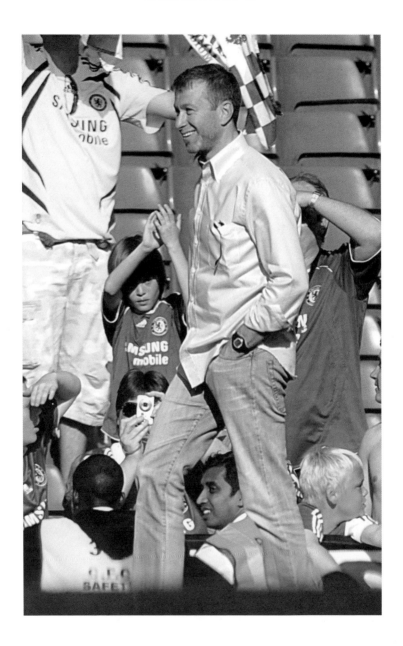

burdening them with would diminish them as both a football and business enterprise.

The following season United came bottom of their Champions League Group, not even qualifying for the Uefa Cup. They were out of Europe by Christmas! How did Glazer react? Did the distant owner sack the ageing manager who had stopped delivering success? No, he allowed the January purchases of defenders Vidic and Evra – not greatly established names and not cheap purchases. United failed to win the League again, coming second to Chelsea, and landed only the Carling Cup, the club's one trophy in two years. Now what did Glazer allow? He supported the £18m purchase of Michael Carrick from Tottenham Hotspur – hardly a bums-on-seats or heart-thumping name – with sixty-four-year-old Sir Alex Ferguson remaining manager.

The following season United won the League and reached the semi-final of the Champions League, and in the next season they won both, beating Chelsea into second place each time.

Abramovich was learning that football and teams go in cycles. Chelsea had just failed to win the Champions League at the peak of their cycle. United had just managed to lift it! Glazer's patience and support had been justified.

The savage coverage that Glazer received was probably something he was prepared for, coming from the United States. The mass coverage Abramovich received on buying Chelsea was a shock. When his oil company Sibneft had completed a major merger, US television news company CNN had covered the event. One story! It was a significant moment in the company's move on to the world stage. CNN!

When Abramovich bought Chelsea, CNN was following his every move for seven days! One whole week! They were camped at Stamford Bridge! He had been launched from unheard-of oligarch to 'Hollywood' style superstar. There would be no more working and living in privacy. Every decision would be scrutinised in the media. It was a completely different culture. Except that he turned his back on it.

But away from the publicity, he got addicted to this drug of football, and of Chelsea Football Club. He loved watching training, he watched Saturday morning youth-team games, he watched a reserve game at Brentford's Griffin Park, he watched Chelsea TV, he watched MUTV, he watched Spanish football, Italian football, all football.

And he worked, and he socialised and he did loads of things we never heard about. And he achieved something for Chelsea Football Club that long-term supporters and long-time players would never have thought possible.

Chelsea chairmen and Chelsea owners were people you never heard from or about. Everyone knew the Mears family was behind the club, and that Joe in particular was an old-school excellent chairman in the 1950s and 1960s. His family successor Brian was a little more high-profile in the 1970s, but he remained a shadow in the background.

Then in 1982 everything changed. The club was in its seventy-seventh year and virtually bankrupt. Enter Ken Bates.

For over twenty years Bates led from the front. He was loud, controversial, ambitious, argumentative, rude, generous, visionary, blind, open-minded, deaf to ideas he wouldn't entertain, he was…well, more complex than most pictures of him have been painted. He was a different generation to Abramovich and much more determined to be in the media but, although neither might think it, maybe they are not so different. They have both worked for and wanted success for Chelsea.

Bates liked the limelight and used it to further the Chelsea cause. Early on, he lost the chance to buy the freehold of Stamford Bridge and had to battle to save the ground. It was a long and bloody battle, and he probably considers winning it against heavy odds his greatest achievement. It wasn't! He then built a new ground. The new Stamford Bridge has a lot of plusses – take any old player on the pitch at half-time as I do and they would give anything to play there now in comparison with the old Stamford Bridge – but with the small pitch, restricted views and surrounding hotels and apartments, maybe it could have been bigger and better.

Bates' greatest achievement as a chairman was to take over a club sliding towards the third tier of English football, reverse its fortunes, and be able to sit and watch the sexiest football south-west London has ever seen – sexier than in the 1960s and 1970s, and sexier than anything that followed: Gullit, Zola, Lebœuf, Desailly, Petrescu, Wise, Di Matteo, Poyet, Hughes, Vialli, Flo...For quite a while there Chelsea were the nation's second favourite team, the team people most wanted to do well after their own, the team everyone said was capable of playing the best football in the land.

But at the height of success, in an appetiser for what was to come with Mourinho, trophy-winning managers Gullit and then Vialli were sacked and the little known Claudio Ranieri was introduced. He took time to adapt and although he was given time and made some good purchases, his high spending never resulted in a trophy. What his high spending did achieve, together with many other factors, was huge debt. By 2002 Chelsea were in trouble and by 2003, having qualified for the Champions League, were ripe for a takeover. Enter Roman Abramovich.

Abramovich had seen his first game in western Europe a few months before, the 4-3 Champions League defeat of Manchester United by Real Madrid at Old Trafford, when Ronaldo hit a stunning hat-trick past Barthez.

Despite all Bates' fevered work, Chelsea never achieved his ultimate ambition. He can't have dreamed that five years later

Abramovich would surpass it.

Ken Bates would have shouted the final word. Had he still been chairman, this would have been his chapter. Roman Abramovich, not the chairman, not on the board, but the owner, passes on the final word.

Quickly, after spending like no other owner or club had spent before, he saw Chelsea win the Premier League twice, the FA Cup, the Carling Cup twice and the FA Community Shield. He saw them lose three Champions League semi-finals, the latter two under Mourinho. And he saw off Mourinho.

Avram Grant took the club to second in the League after a difficult start under Mourinho, and he took them to a penalty-kick short of winning the Champions League. In his home city Moscow, Abramovich saw Manchester United beat Chelsea 6-5 on penalties in a splendid Champions League Final. He then saw off Grant.

As the media frenzied over who would be the new manager, Chelsea said little and Abramovich, of course, revealed nothing. Perhaps the reason that the media was constantly so wide of the mark in its speculation was that Abramovich was making sure this was done his way – without publicity. He knew now how to run the show for the best.

Luiz Felipe Scolari was always the number one target but, for the most part, not the media favourite for the job. Other people got hounded in the speculation. Yet, as soon as announced, he was acknowledged as amongst the world's very best, a Chelsea - or Abramovich - coup.

For twenty years Ken Bates regularly stated he wanted to make Chelsea the Manchester United of the south. He failed. In five years, with his success and his moving of managers, Abramovich has made Chelsea the Real Madrid of the north!

That is the final word. For now!

ALSO AVAILABLE IN THE SERIES